Thoughtful Teachers, Thoughtful Learners

A Guide to Helping Adolescents
Think Critically

NORMAN J. UNRAU

Pippin Publishing

Copyright © 1997 by Pippin Publishing Corporation
P.O. Box 242
Don Mills
Ontario M3C 2S2
www.pippinpub.com

All rights reserved. No part of this publication may be
reproduced or transmitted in any form or by any means,
electronic, mechanical, or otherwise, including photocopying
and recording, or stored in any retrieval system
without permission in writing from the publisher.

Edited by Dyanne Rivers
Designed by John Zehethofer
Printed and bound in Canada by Marquis Book Printing Inc.

We acknowledge the assistance of the OMDC Book Fund, an initiative
of Ontario Media Development Corporation.

Canadian Cataloguing in Publication Data

Unrau, Norman
    Thoughtful teachers, thoughtful learners:
a guide to helping adolescents think critically

(The Pippin teacher's library)
Includes bibliographical references.
ISBN 0-88751-082-5

1. Critical thinking - Study and teaching. 2. Inter-
disciplinary approach in education. I. Title. II. Series.

LB1590.3.U57 1997   370.15′2   C97-930876-3

10   9   8   7   6   5   4   3   2

CONTENTS

. . . .

INTRODUCTION

Al had taught English for 21 years—seven in a junior high and 14 at Adams High School. Students liked his enthusiasm and humor. Parents maneuvered their children into his classes. He had a reputation for being creative and challenging, and for taking a personal interest in the students in his classes.

Despite his apparent success, though, Al had never been entirely satisfied with teaching. Three years into his career, he began browsing through law school catalogues. After 10 years, he dreamed of opening a restaurant. After 16 years, he considered getting a real estate license. Then, he began figuring out how he would get along on his retirement checks. Al had become cynical about making changes in his school. What had been meaningful and important to him—challenging students to think about what they say, read and write—was drowning in routine. Still, the part of Al that loved teaching always won out over the part that wanted to leave the profession behind.

Al's malaise deepened when a new principal was appointed in response to parental nagging about the academic decline of Adams High. His job? To "spearhead reform." Unfortunately, few teachers trusted the new principal's leadership. Many felt he ignored their input and were convinced that the school was floundering.

Within Al, the cynic fought with the optimist. The time for the school's re-accreditation was at hand, and a team of evaluators would soon visit Adams. Faculty members were meeting to write course descriptions, sort through opinion surveys completed by both students and parents, and renego-tiate—and perhaps renew—education at Adams. Although Al often saw this process as a joke, part of him hoped that some-thing would come of it.

During one of many lunch-hour accreditation meetings, Al sat with his colleagues in Barbara's classroom. Al admired Barbara, the chair of his department. She could stir fierce discussions among her students, and she could also annoy the principal when he tried to flex his muscle without consulting the staff.

Barbara's calendar read Tuesday, April 19, the date the "shot heard round the world" was fired in Concord, Massa-chusetts. Maybe it's time for another revolt, Al thought.

Al listened as Maria, a teacher at Adams for 10 years, talked about the principal's plans for restructuring the school.

"After all these meetings, shouldn't we have some sense of direction?" Maria asked.

"Maybe we shouldn't expect the principal to set our direc-tion," Al suggested.

"Don't we have a pretty good idea of where we're going already?" asked Mark, who had turned to teaching 12 years before.

"That's true, but we don't really have anything that holds us together, gives us a sense of direction," Al said. "Instead of each of us going this way or that, couldn't we have some kind of unifying vision? Something that would give us a purpose in common?"

"What do you have in mind?" Barbara asked.

"I'm not sure, Barbara, but it seems to me that the faculty doesn't share values that guide our decisions about what or how to teach."

"We're all pretty independent, Al," said Mark. "We pretty much always have been. Individuals, I mean."

"But if we could share some sort of educational ideal, some-thing that would hold us together...know what I mean?"

"What kind of ideal?" Mark asked.

"What about a common goal? Like teaching students to think—not just take in information, but transform it into something meaningful. Students tell me they're learning stuff, but they don't know why or what it's worth or how it relates to their lives. Of course, that's not true in our department."

"Right. We're doing great. It's the other departments that need help," Barbara quipped.

"All joking aside, that's something I hear about every department. So, I suggest we think about the ideal of the critical thinker," Al paused to read the faces of his colleagues. "A critical thinker. You know, someone who uses reason to guide decision-making and thinks through his or her beliefs. I mean are we preparing these kids for life—right now, and after they graduate? What are we doing to help them make better decisions? Are they going on impulse or what?"

"Mostly impulse," Maria said acerbically.

"Mostly," Al echoed. "But students need some skills to get through school. To know how to function at work. Just memorizing won't do. Even if we could get them to read tons of literature—to know all there is about history, science, math—that wouldn't do it. Information alone isn't enough. If we could share a vision about teaching thinking..."

"What kind of vision?" Barbara asked

"A vision based on the development of critical thinking, a view that puts meaningful reflection on what is learned ahead of storing information and passing tests."

"We've talked about doing critical thinking in social studies," said Maria, "but I'm confused. One teacher told me he just tells students there's a difference between facts and opinions. I don't think that's what you're talking about, Al. Is it?"

"I'm not sure what we should decide it is," Al said, "but I do think that if we're going to develop a common vision, an ideal, we'll need to agree on what critical thinking means. Otherwise..."

"Otherwise, we'll all go in our own directions—just as Maria said is happening in social studies," Barbara finished the sentence for him.

"What would the purposes of this be, Al?" asked Mark.

"We'd have to talk about that, too. We just don't have any common purpose that holds us together as a community."

"To get through the week," Maria said.

"To get our students into college if they want to go," Barbara added.

"But why go to college? Why learn anything?" Al asked. "I don't think I get my students to reflect on decisions. To think about what they do—or should do."

Barbara studied Al. "Let's say we go with your educational ideal," she said. "An ideal isn't enough. We need to know how we're going to realize that ideal—or we'll be right back to the way we're doing things now. So, how do we build reflective learners?"

"I don't think that's going to be easy. First, we've got to be reflective, critical thinkers ourselves—or we've got to move in that direction. Do we want every faculty meeting to be a batch of announcements on a sheet of paper? Or do we want to play a central role in the decisions that count in making us what we are?"

"Or do we ignore it all, go into our own classrooms, and do what we want?" Mark added.

"We do it together. It can't be done by one of us deciding to teach for thinking and telling the rest what to do. We've got to persuade the faculty that this vision is worth working toward. That it will change the way we teach and the way students learn. We're going to have to design a program that will move us from where we are to where we want to be."

"So, let's say we design a curriculum to teach thinking across departments," Mark said. "How do we know it's going to work? What if parents or school board members start asking us for evidence that this new approach teaches students to think better? Is there any research backing up this ideal we're talking about?"

"Oh, who cares about the research, Mark? Let's get this going if we're going to do it," Maria said. "If we wait around for researchers to tell us everything, we'll never do anything. Let's just do it!"

Al wasn't surprised by Maria's enthusiasm. He only hoped he could convince her of the importance of a program based on both passion and reason. "We have to find some way to evaluate what we're going to do and be ready to change if it's not working. We need the evaluation part of this—or it may look like just another fancy fad."

"Should we recommend integrating critical thinking into our courses over the next few years?" Barbara asked.

"If we do that, the evaluation committee will write it into its report, and there goes some of our freedom," Mark grimaced. He paused, looking at Al. "But maybe we'll gain some kind of solidarity through...through what?"

"Sharing an ideal," said Maria.

"Exactly," said Mark.

"Then it's agreed that we'll work on it?" Barbara asked.

Nods from Maria and Mark accompanied the bell signaling the end of lunch. Al left the meeting feeling that the first shot in an educational revolution had been fired. But he also knew that unity over the ideal was many skirmishes away.

. . . .

Al is a fictional teacher. But this hypothetical story of a dream for change may not, after all, be so hypothetical. Over the last few years, there have been similar conversations about critical thinking among many groups of fellow-teachers in several different disciplines and at most grade levels.

Many among us, even those who are well-informed and experienced, may not have had a chance to think through our conceptions of "critical thinking." We may not have talked to colleagues about the content that constitutes a critical thinking curriculum. Many of us are interested in discovering or designing strategies for integrating critical thinking into the curriculum, but have no time to do this. And, perhaps most important, many of us are well along the road to understanding that analytical skills and knowledge won't be enough — that a disposition to seek reasons and a means to hold knowledge and belief in a flexible way are also essential.

As an introduction to teaching for thinking, *Thoughtful Teachers, Thoughtful Learners* is intended to stimulate inquiry among those of us who have begun to think about re-envisioning teaching with a focus on developing reflective learners and critical thinkers. Perhaps it will awaken similar thoughts in those of us who are searching for a new way to give our teaching greater meaning to both ourselves and our students.

A variety of purposes guided the writing of this book:

— To help us enable students to discover and reflect upon how they think and what they do when they engage in argumentative discourse in both everyday life and academic settings.
— To encourage us to foster the growth of rational and reflective thinking and to focus instruction on the ideal of encouraging critical thought.

— To provide a definition of critical thinking that can be used to promote the use of reason and reflection while learning.
— To develop an appreciation of the social contexts of thought and the influence of culture on thinking.
— To help us understand the cognitive and affective backgrounds that shape thinking.
— To explore strategies that we can use to develop reflection on thinking and the thinking process and to enhance thoughtful learning.
— To help us become skillful at guiding discussions that encourage discovery and asking questions that promote inquiry.
— To provide us with a theoretical framework for critical thinking and the development of reflective learners that can be used as a guide for designing curriculum.
— To demonstrate how we can help our students learn to read between the lines in order to discover assumptions, values, beliefs, and attitudes that may be embedded in spoken or written communication.
— To provide us with a means of nurturing in students the ability to compose persuasive texts, to construct thesis statements, to consider alternative viewpoints, and to appreciate the effects of bias.
— To help us and our students discover and appreciate that meanings are perpetually negotiable.
— To provide information about resources, such as books, journals and professional organizations, that can help foster further growth in our understanding and knowledge of critical thinking and the development of reflective learners.

The first chapter examines critical thinking and how it can guide the growth of reflective reasoning. The second explores the reasons teaching thinking is a good idea. It also presents lesson planning guidelines that can be used to integrate the teaching of thinking into a curriculum and presents a portfolio method for assessing the growth of thinking. The chapter titled "Thinking through Talking" introduces activities designed to enable us and our students to learn more about argument and the way we use language in argumentative discourse. This chapter also explores methods of improving classroom discussion and questioning tactics.

The next chapter, "Thinking through Reading," presents a brief overview of the reading process and a set of reader-based response strategies designed to guide reflective reading and the reasoned analysis of arguments. The fifth chapter, "Thinking through Reading with TASK," outlines TASK—thesis-analysis-synthesis key—a procedure designed to help students read arguments more reflectively by examining both the claims an author makes and the evidence used to support these claims. The sixth chapter, "Thinking through Writing," explains tactics that help guide students toward writing more reflectively. The final chapter, "Thinking through Writing with TASK," demonstrates how the TASK procedure can help students write their own arguments.

The teachers at Adams High are revisited briefly in the epilogue and the book concludes with resources and references that can be used to help develop a critical thinking curriculum.

. . . .

WHAT IS

CRITICAL THINKING?

Those who have kept watch on the critical thinking movement have observed an evolution in both its theory and practice. Some observers, such as Richard Paul, suggest that it has progressed in waves.

Beginning in the early 1970s, the first wave focused narrowly on the theory of logic and the techniques of argument. Practitioners developed stand-alone courses in critical thinking, based on formal or informal logic. In these courses, teachers often encouraged students to dismantle and examine the structure of arguments, but made little reference to a larger context and provided little support for transferring analytical techniques beyond the classroom.

The second wave, which arose in the mid-1980s, was marked by diversity in theory, purpose and practice. Though more comprehensive than the first wave, this wave was also more diffuse and lacked a common core of agreements about logic and reason in which to ground critical thinking. Nevertheless, an understanding of the importance of critical thinking began to spread beyond the academic world to other domains, such as business, the media, parenting and our emotional lives. Although the teaching of critical thinking skills began to show up on school curriculums, no conceptual foundation grounded this work across the curriculum.

If a third wave can be detected on the horizon, it might be marked by a balance between close scrutiny of thought and broad inclusiveness, while incorporating discoveries from cognitive science. The concept of critical thinking presented in this book is intended to move toward this kind of integration and balance—toward the swelling of a new wave in critical thinking.

Integrating critical thinking into school curriculums is important for many reasons. For example, although we're flooded with information, we often have difficulty transforming it into useful knowledge. As we watch TV, go to movies, listen to the radio, connect with the WorldWide Web, and read newspapers, magazines and books, we are often urged to buy all sorts of products. But evaluating our choices as consumers, whether these involve buying a car, purchasing life insurance, or selecting an investment, requires reasoned thinking.

We also need to think reflectively about our government. To function effectively, democracies require informed deliberation on issues that affect individuals, communities and nations. The survival of our society depends on a knowledgeable electorate that has access to a free flow of information in order to test opinions, question convictions and make thoughtful decisions.

The ability to think critically is just as important in school. No matter what the field, the ability to think critically enables students to recognize and construct sound arguments and hypotheses, and evaluate conclusions. As a result, critical thinking needs to pervade every aspect of the curriculum in every subject area.

When I first ventured into developing critical thinking as a focus for instruction, the first wave of the movement, with its emphasis on rigorously analyzing arguments, was cresting. As its influence began to expand, however, the meaning of critical thinking became less focused and more elusive. I recall groping to clarify the term, a process that was much like trying to capture big floating bubbles in a butterfly net.

In my search for clarity, I learned about promising programs to enhance critical thinking in many domains, an indication perhaps of the second wave's trend toward diversity. I read books, many of which are listed under Additional Reading in "Resources," intended to help encourage students to think critically and apply this skill in various fields. I listened and talked to educators who had thought and written about critical thinking. And I began to serve on curriculum and staff development committees that focused on teaching thinking.

Eventually, I began to construct and reconstruct my own concept of critical thinking. As I read and continue to learn more about critical thinking, I've come to view it as a process, a network of dispositions, and an outlook—all of which are framed in a social context.

Critical Thinking: A Process

When we hear the word "critical," various meanings come to mind. It can mean essential, as in "Al's contribution was critical to the success of the program." It can also mean fault-finding, sarcastic, carping or backbiting, as in "Every time she talks about the principal, she's critical."

When "critical" is paired with "thinker," however, an entirely different meaning is suggested. A critical thinker is closer to a critic, in the original Greek and Latin sense of the word—someone who is able to discern or judge.

What is critical thinking, then? Influenced by the work of Robert Ennis, I define it as a process of reasoned reflection on the meaning of claims about what to believe or what to do. It may be worthwhile to examine this definition phrase by phrase.

REASONED REFLECTION...

To say that critical thinking requires reasoned reflection suggests that some form of reasoning occurs when a thinker reflects upon statements. It also suggests that before we embrace a claim, we're going to look for good reasons to do so.

When reflecting on the validity of a claim, we bring many rational resources to bear. These include logic, evidence, and our knowledge of fallacies, probability and statistics, as well as a variety of other guidelines for determining the reasonableness of a statement. Modifying Plato's famous adage that the unexamined life is not worth living, I'd say that the unexamined claim is not worth claiming.

The notion that critical thinking entails rational reflection implies that irrational processes are suspect. Intuition, gut-level feelings, dogmatic assertions, and it's-true-because-I-say-so statements don't cut it in the realm of rational reflection. This is not to say that critical thinkers must banish intuition and emotion—as if they could or should! These less rational aspects of decision-making exercise enormous psychological power. However, they should be inspected in the

14

bright light of reason rather than left to influence the darker chambers of the mind.

It's worth noting that the word "reflection" doesn't imply that critical thinking is always re-active. Critical thinking also occurs when we form a claim designed to avert potential crises. If we were unable to take steps to avoid these, our ability to think critically wouldn't be of much use.

...ON THE MEANING OF CLAIMS...

A claim is a unit of meaning or knowledge. When gold miners, for example, stake a claim, they set out the boundaries of a site to which they have a right. In a sense, when we make a claim, we verbally stake out a site in the world. We announce what we believe to be true about some aspect of the world.

Whenever we make, hear or read claims, we construct a meaning for them; in other words, when we engage in reasoned reflection on claims, we do so on the basis of the meaning or meanings we have constructed. As a unit of meaning, a claim may be a proposition, an assertion, a judgment, a solution to a dilemma, or a declaration of belief.

Most arguments consist of a small but hard-working set of claim types that either constitute the core assertion—the thesis—of an argument or convey supporting reasons and evidence. We can make claims about what we think is true (fact or knowledge claims), what causes something (causal claims), what is likely to happen (predictive claims), what is good (evaluative claims), what is right (moral claims), or what ought to be done (policy claims). While most claims fall into one of these categories, some overlap and are not as easily pigeonholed (mixed claims).

Fact or knowledge claims state that something is true (e.g., trees grow; blood carries oxygen to cells of the body). Even scientists, however, must sometimes revise or drop broadly accepted truths. Other fact claims change with time (e.g., Harriet lives on Elm Street—she may move to Oak Street). In a world of rapidly expanding and changing knowledge, fact claims are probably best viewed as working hypotheses that require constant verification to maintain their status as truth.

Causal claims assert that something caused something else to happen (e.g., children fail in school because they don't find it meaningful; higher interest rates caused the recession). Although causal claims are part of the same family as fact claims—they make a statement about how things work and require evidence to verify them—they live in a different house.

Predictive claims foretell an event (e.g., this generation of kids will bring our country to ruin; Quebec's economy will suffer if it separates from Canada). These are predictive claims because they predict that something will happen in the future. Obviously, predictions can be incorrect.

When making predictive claims, we use our perception of cause-and-effect patterns to predict future events. We speculate about what will happen in the future based upon what appeared to have been the case in the past or what appears to be the case in the present. When predictive claims are founded on weak observations or unsound cause-and-effect relationships, the likelihood that the prediction will come true is substantially diminished.

Evaluative claims assert the quality, worth or value of something, such as a work of art, an event, a company, a program or a person (e.g., Harley Davidson makes the finest motorcycle; Shakespeare was the world's greatest poet).

Moral claims are judgments about the rightness or wrongness, or the goodness or evil, of behavior (e.g., capital punishment must be abolished; murder is wrong). Moral claims are, however, usually open to debate; for example, if a grief-stricken father shoots his three-year-old daughter, who has been in a coma out of which she is never expected to emerge, he has committed a crime—but has he committed an immoral act? Some may conclude that this "mercy killing" was moral— even though it was illegal and punishable by imprisonment or even death.

Policy claims offer a solution to a problem. And because problems sprout like dandelions in summer, we hear lots of policy claims. Typically, policy claims present a program for correcting an injustice or filling a need (e.g., focusing on the three Rs will stem "the rising tide of mediocrity" in schools). Because people propose policy claims based on their perception of problems and because people see things differently, contradictory policy claims are common. For example, a politician might see industrial growth as the solution to the problems of an economically disadvantaged region, while environmentalists might propose creating a national park in the area.

Mixed claims are claims that fit into more than one of the previous categories. When this happens, it's often because one type of claim implies another. A policy claim, for example, may be proposed because its author believes it's morally sound, thus basing a policy claim on a moral one. For example, a newspaper editorial recently rejected the idea of creating a rating system to assess the lyrics of popular songs. In essence, it made an evaluative claim based on a policy claim that suggested rating popular songs. This policy claim was in turn based on the moral claim that parents have the right to protect their children against "corrupting" influences. By the way, the editorial also made an alternative policy claim—that the best way for parents to prevent children from being influenced by raunchy lyrics is to increase their involvement with them.

A single sentence may contain several claims, each of which represents knowledge of different kinds or expresses our feelings in the form of an attitude, value or belief. Our capacity to break down complex sentences into smaller units of meaning, or claims, contributes a great deal to the development of reflective thinking. Essential to this development is our ability to examine claims rationally, something we couldn't do effectively if we couldn't separate complicated, connected statements into smaller units of meaning.

One of the reasons I describe critical thinking as reasoned reflection on the *meaning* of claims is that meaning is often understood differently by different interpreters. Critical thinking is an interpretive process. Critical thinkers do not reproduce knowledge; they use their minds to interpret all kinds of symbolic forms. In addition to printed texts, these forms may include movies, dance, lectures, conversations, music and so on. Rather than accepting received wisdom, critical thinkers construct new understandings that can stand up to reflection and reasoned examination.

...ABOUT WHAT TO BELIEVE OR WHAT TO DO

The claims that we make and reflect upon are usually about what to believe or what to do. What we believe can include everything from everyday facts that we consider immutable and true (e.g., water freezes) to the conviction that each of us will attain immortality. We all hold a variety of beliefs about our world, our selves and our destiny.

While what we believe and what we do are closely connected, we can reflect rationally on a wide range of possible
actions, just as we can ponder a wide range of beliefs. We can
rationally examine what to do about our personal lives, our
professional or vocational futures, our economic woes, or our
interest in losing 10 pounds.

Critical Thinking: A Network of Dispositions

Capable, resourceful and knowledgeable people don't necessarily use their abilities, resources or knowledge to examine
claims rationally. They may believe something without question or examination, and they may act on their beliefs without
thoughtfully reflecting on their actions—or the consequences.
To think critically, we must be equipped with more than skills,
knowledge and resources.

We also need a disposition—or inclination—to think critically. We need to be favorably disposed toward the idea of
engaging in reasonable thinking, a trait that increases the
likelihood that we will actually do it. It's worth noting that
even those who possess the resources and the inclination to
think critically may experience episodes of what Keith Stanovich calls dysrationalia—times when our ability to engage
our rational capacity or intelligence is impaired. Unfortunately, these episodes can occur at moments when becoming
rationally engaged is extremely important.

In fact, a disposition to think critically involves a variety of
dispositions to do specific things. I think of these as a network
that, when fully engaged, is likely to result in productive
critical thinking. This network includes a disposition to:

— Seek reasons with rational rigor.
— Imagine alternative solutions and perspectives.
— Make an effort and persevere in acquiring and integrat-
   ing knowledge.
— Be intellectually playful.
— Plan.
— Acquire, apply and evaluate the effectiveness of strate-
   gies.
— Evaluate the consequences of beliefs, decisions and ac-
   tions.

— Reflect on one's own thinking and that of others in order to gain knowledge of oneself and others.

It may be surprising to find a disposition to be intellectually playful included on this list. It's important to understand, however, that productive critical thinkers are game for trying out new ideas and amused by the serious sport of thought. This playfulness is often evident when people frame problems creatively, as did Albert Einstein, and when we generate "what if..." scenarios. It does not imply irresponsibility; on the contrary, it reflects an imaginative commitment to dialogue and involves flexibility, resilience and the ability to juggle ideas.

It may be far less surprising to find that the list includes a disposition to reflect on one's own thinking and that of others. This is important because, for some people, "winning" an argument—and displaying their thinking abilities—is the most important goal. These people use their considerable thinking skills to vehemently defend their own positions and attack those of others. Richard Paul calls this critical thinking in the "weak sense." "Strong-sense" critical thinkers are open to reviewing their own positions and sympathetically exploring those of others. Clearly, teachers are interested in encouraging students to become critical thinkers in the strong sense.

A disposition to think critically involves far more than applying bits of knowledge or other resources from time to time in order to examine specific claims. It involves a network of inclinations, sensitivities and capabilities that pervade our everyday thinking. In an ideal world, all of us would activate every aspect of this network all the time. Few, if any, of us are capable of doing this, however. Perhaps the best that can be said is that proficient thinkers activate more of these dispositions more of the time than less careful thinkers.

Critical Thinking: A Transformative Outlook

This third dimension of critical thinking views all claims as open to examination and challenge. No claim is as solid as a rock, and any claim is capable not only of being transformed by us but also of transforming us.

In addition to understanding that critical thought involves a network of dispositions that pervades everyday life, teachers need to encourage students to adopt an outlook that encompasses the possibility that apparently solid facts and immutable beliefs may change. Even so-called foundational truths may be modified.

From this perspective, the conclusions we reach are but temporary resting stations on a journey. Even when we seem to recognize an absolute certainty, we need to remind ourselves that granite mountains can erode and disappear. Critical thinkers do not assume that they will eventually discover an eternal foundation upon which to build enduring truths.

THE LIMITS OF SCIENCE

In the past, many thinkers and teachers regarded the so-called scientific method as the ideal guide to the development of critical thinking because it requires the production of observable and verifiable evidence to prove hypotheses. If no scientific evidence can be produced, a hypothesis must be changed and testing must start again. This is certainly a transformative process.

Many thinkers have now begun to doubt the truth-yielding capacity of the scientific method, however. While this method requires us to produce evidence to support a hypothesis, which is reasonable, it also contributes to the growth of theories that may influence the way we interpret what we see. As a result, the very theory that we induce from an inquiry may distort what we perceive when we apply it.

For example, imagine that biologists, part of an interplanetary research team, have landed on a planet called Novavita. The animals they see are unfamiliar. Classifying and labeling them is their job.

The biologists observe that one of the animals is covered with orange-spotted blue bumps. They also notice that these creatures seem to greet one another with a noise that sounds like "frump." As a result, they decide to call them frumpers. This decision is important because, as the biologists continue their task, their observations will be influenced by the fact that they've already created a category identified as frumpers.

One day, a colleague notices that many of the frumpers don't make any noise at all. Not a sound. They look like frumpers; they walk like frumpers; they eat like frumpers. But they're different. Upon closer inspection, another difference becomes obvious. These creatures also have a tiny yellow dot at the end of their tails. Clearly they aren't frumpers. A new category will need to be created.

In *The Structure of Scientific Revolutions*, Thomas Kuhn documented a process by which changes in scientific theories—which he called paradigm shifts—occurred because the results of experimental research forced a restructuring of scientific principles. In these instances, the traditional principles—or hypotheses—couldn't explain the new results—or evidence. Kuhn also pointed out that a scientific community's shared beliefs in a theory or prevailing paradigm can influence the way evidence is interpreted.

A further drawback of the scientific method is that its purportedly objective perspective can't be applied in every situation. Can the scientific method help make policy decisions on welfare, health or crime-prevention programs? Can it be used to evaluate films, novels and paintings? Some judgments, especially those that involve interpreting objects or events, can't be made on the basis of objective measurement criteria. For example, no experiment could help us decide whether Picasso's *Guernica* or Rembrandt's *Aristotle Contemplating the Bust of Homer* is the better painting.

The scientific method also comes up short as a way of dealing with the social and political worlds. In these worlds, decisions about what to do are often made on the basis of individual interpretations and subjective understandings that can't be tested experimentally. For example, how are we, as citizens, to interpret history in a way that informs our judgments about future decisions?

Some philosophers, such as A.J. Ayer, have argued that we should not expect to gather useful information by applying the methods of empirical science to questions of worth. But when an individual or a community decides to investigate something, whether this is the mating behavior of butterflies or the destructiveness of a neutron bomb, someone's value system has been engaged in deciding what is to be investigated. We might even say that any decision to purposely apply the scientific method involves an implicit assessment of worth.

Clearly, the scientific method has had—and will continue to have—a profound effect on human affairs, despite the fact that its usefulness is limited in many situations.

To understand that conclusions are but temporary resting places, it helps to envision the process of interpreting and reinterpreting, of understanding and re-understanding, as a cycle of meanings, sometimes called the hermeneutic circle.

Broadly speaking, hermeneutics is the study of meanings or interpretations. For some time, philosophers have embraced the idea that our minds are interpretive agents in a world of signs and symbols. Whenever we draw meaning from something, we bring to it our own personal background of knowledge and beliefs. For example, several students may read T.S. Eliot's *The Waste Land* and each may interpret it differently. In assigning meaning to something, we accept that others will construct their own meanings, which may differ from ours, that no one person has access to the truth, and that we will discuss rationally the validity of our interpretations.

Critical thinkers with a transformative outlook recognize that the quest for valid interpretations is a recursive, circular activity. It is a cycle of meanings. These meanings are constructed from continuing interactions between hypothesis and evidence, the whole and its parts, theory and perception, and the general and the specific. When we think, these apparently discrete interactions often parallel or complement one another. Furthermore, they occur in the context of language, which has enormous power to influence our interpretations because it frames every interpretive act.

For example, when we interpret a text, the meanings we construct for the whole influence our interpretation of its parts, while our understanding of the parts shapes our interpretation of the whole. Take *The Waste Land*, for example. Our overall interpretation of the poem's meaning may influence the way we interpret specific symbolic elements within it. At the same time, our interpretation of specific symbolic elements within the poem influences our interpretation of its overall meaning.

Similarly, as we learn more about particular cases or specific details in a domain of knowledge, our new knowledge is likely to change the generalizations we have constructed on the basis of previous observations or discoveries. Thus, we are always in a cycle in which specific information and events influence the generalizations we induce and the generalizations we induce influence our perceptions of new specific information and events.

It's worth noting that the scientific method, which involves forming and testing hypotheses, plays an important role in the circle of meanings. When thinkers test a hypothesis by applying new evidence to it, they may be comparing the whole theory to its supporting parts or vice versa.

The usefulness and power of the scientific method is not diminished when it is seen within the larger framework of a cycle of meanings. As a result, adopting the hermeneutic circle as a model that explains how thinking occurs does not mean abandoning the reason and rationality of the scientific method. It does not suggest that relativity reigns supreme, that anything goes, or that a claim is valid just because someone says so. On the contrary, claims must be open to confirmation and refutation as knowledge grows. The quest involves discovering not only good reasons to hold claims, but also good reasons to modify or even abandon them.

Critical Thinking: The Social Context

When we reflect on a claim, we don't bring our knowledge and beliefs to bear in isolation. We always activate these in a social context. Because knowledge, beliefs and the social context are so dependent on one another, distinguishing among them is like trying to separate a swamp from the water in it; something important gets lost in the process. Nevertheless, I'll treat each of these features distinctly while acknowledging that, in the swamps of real life, they're pretty much inseparable.

KNOWLEDGE

Some educators, including John McPeak and E.D. Hirsch Jr., have argued that critical thinking skills are not necessarily transferable. Rather than teaching critical thinking, therefore, teachers should focus on helping students gain as deep a knowledge of specific subjects as possible.

I believe that approaches to inquiry and dispositions learned in one domain will transfer to others, especially if we teach with the possibility of this transfer in mind and encourage the integration of critical thinking across the disciplines. At the same time, I also believe that we must help students acquire as much knowledge as possible because the more they know, the more knowledge they will be able to apply as they reason reflectively about claims, both in school and out.

Schema theory helps us understand how background knowledge shapes our thinking. In simple terms, a schema is a diagrammatic representation of a structure. When the term is applied to knowledge, it refers to a hypothesized mental structure that represents knowledge gained and stored in our long-term memory. These memory structures or schemata—the plural of schema—can be viewed as knowledge modules or networks, each of which helps us organize a specific class of concepts formed as a result of experiences. It sometimes helps to think of each schema as a cluster of related claims.

Many kinds of knowledge, including world, procedural, metacognitive and personal knowledge, may be stored as schemata. In our minds, we construct schemata in many sizes—from the simple image activated when we read the word "robin" to the complex arrays of information associated with a word like "education." Whether each schema is a simple unit of knowledge or a vast network of information, it tends to lie dormant in our memory until it is activated when we talk, listen, read, write or think critically.

When activated, schemata guide the way our thought processes behave when we encounter new information. If this information fits the pattern of existing schemata, these schemata can control the process we use to make meaning. This is often helpful. Schemata help us search our memories, make inferences, reorganize information, summarize and accomplish many of our daily tasks. For example, most of us have constructed a schema for grocery stores that is activated when we go shopping. Even when we enter an unfamiliar store, we have a pretty good idea of where to look for milk, tomatoes, Cheerios, chicken breasts and the other items on our shopping list, as well as how to negotiate the checkout counter.

Using existing schemata to guide our thought processes and make meaning can also be a hindrance, however. Doing so can lead us to overlook important information because it doesn't fit an expected pattern, or distort information to force it to fit existing patterns. Remember how the frumper schema changed?

It can also lead us to miss important interpretations. If, for example, readers of *The Adventures of Huckleberry Finn* activate an adventure-story schema and read the book only as a series of adventures, they may miss its satirical elements.

While we certainly need to be aware of the power of schemata to restrict our thinking, we also need to be aware that they provide valuable reservoirs of information that help us build new knowledge structures. When we encounter new information, we don't create a new schema; rather, we take chunks of knowledge from existing schemata, recombine them, and emerge with new knowledge structures that represent novel experiences and original thinking.

BELIEFS

Critical thinking involves examining claims to decide what to believe. When we do this, we activate not only our background knowledge in the form of schemata but also our existing beliefs.

Beliefs come in many forms. They may include a variety of fact claims as well as all sorts of other claims. They influence our understanding of causes, the predictions we make, the way we evaluate things, our morals and our policies.

Beliefs manifest themselves as convictions, opinions and assumptions. Convictions often guide life decisions. For example, someone may believe that dedicating himself to serving others gives life meaning. Opinions may lead us to say that football is the most exciting sport. Assumptions may shape our thinking even when we're not fully aware of this, as occurs when underlying theories influence our perceptions. In these ways, our beliefs form a context for critical thinking.

It's worth noting that belief in a claim isn't necessarily an either-or, yes-or-no deal. We might be convinced that 1 + 1 = 2 or that robins fly, but even in mathematics, especially in the domain of probability, people accept fact claims with varying degrees of belief. Researchers, for example, customarily agree that a claim is valid if the condition it describes occurs 95 times out of 100. Here are two examples of fact claims that individuals may believe to varying degrees:

— Ghosts exist.
— Taxes will be collected next year.

To ascertain whether we believe these statements, we bring evidence and reason to bear. While the statement about taxes

25

is probably pretty sound, a belief in ghosts might be less solid. Many of us have trouble accepting evidence that phantoms exist. Others, however, might not want to completely close the door on this belief, especially because the ghosts could end up coming right through it anyway.

Unless we're prone to thinking in absolutes, there are probably also variations in the degree to which we believe evaluative claims. Consider this judgment: "Plato said everything important there is to say about philosophy." Sounds interesting, but we know that ideas of what is important in the domain of philosophy can vary dramatically. The degree to which we agree with this opinion may depend on the extent of evidence and reasoning that we can find to support it. An expert in the field who is obsessed with Plato's genius might believe in this claim to a high degree. A logical positivist or an advocate of the scientific method might not believe in it at all.

Others may have a different problem altogether. Although they may admire Plato, they may recognize that they don't know enough about philosophy to assess the accuracy of the claim. Modifying it to say "Plato said much that is of importance in the field of philosophy" might make more of them inclined to believe it.

In addition to varying from weak to strong, our belief in claims of all kinds may change with experience, evidence and reasoning. This is evident if we examine the statement that the earth is the center of the universe, a fact claim that was widely accepted until Nicolaus Copernicus demoted our planet. A more contemporary example is the fact claim that the universe is composed of about 10 billion galaxies. This is a lot. Enough to keep us up all night counting them—and enough to encourage a belief that life in some form is likely to exist on at least one of the planets in one of those galaxies. But wait! With the better eyes of the Hubble Space Telescope, astronomers now suggest that 50 billion galaxies is a more accurate estimate. This increases by many times the likelihood that another planet in one of these galaxies is capable of sustaining life, an increase in probabilities that may also magnify a person's belief in extra-terrestrial life.

Not all beliefs are easy to examine—or change. Some people may hold beliefs, such as in the possibility of extra-terrestrial life or even ghosts, that they're unwilling to subject to reasoned reflection. When working in the context of students' belief system, teachers must be very sensitive to this reluctance. It isn't unusual to encounter people who believe they have a right to an unexamined opinion and who will claim, "I have a right to my opinion and nothing's going to change that." By this, they may mean that they have both a right to their opinions and a right to hold them unexamined.

Nevertheless, teachers do need to cultivate contexts in which claims and beliefs of all kinds can be explored. After all, we ought to be able to examine claims such as "sloth is better than gluttony"—if we're not overcome by lethargy first—to discover the degree to which we believe them.

Our knowledge of and beliefs about claims of all kinds develop in a social context. When we learn, either directly or indirectly, we tend to do so mostly as a result of social interactions. Although the underlying capacity of human beings to acquire language may be innate, we learn our particular language and acquire a bounty of cultural knowledge through social exchanges that take place within our families and communities. These interactions shape the way we construct our worlds, reach understandings about our institutions, and learn about ourselves and others. They shape our beliefs and our actions.

Furthermore, when we think, we do so in social contexts. These contexts include the classroom, the living room, and the workroom. We think in the social contexts of friendships, student-teacher relationships, employer-employee associations, and so on.

Conclusion

Proficient critical thinkers are disposed to engage in a process of rational reflection on the meaning of claims that are constantly evolving in cycles of reasoned inquiry that take place in the context of knowledge and beliefs that are shaped by social interactions. During these cycles, we seek the best reasons we can to sustain our claims.

How can teachers of all subjects establish conditions that encourage students to become critical thinkers? This question is explored in the next chapter.

. . . .

PLANNING TO TEACH

CRITICAL THINKING

Whenthey first face the task of designing lessons
on their own, student teachers sometimes ask, "Where do I
start?" Because deciding on a starting point often requires us
to figure out where we plan to end up, I routinely suggest that
they start by thinking about their goals. These may include the
course content they wish to cover, the kinds of thinking they
wish to promote, and even the kinds of growth they wish to
see in themselves.

Following my own advice, then, this chapter begins by
discussing goals for teaching critical thinking. Then, because
assessment is a continuing process that is inextricably linked
to the goals we set, a method of assessing students' progress
toward achieving these goals is introduced. With this groundwork laid, the nuts and bolts of the planning process can be
discussed. This material includes an exploration of lesson-
planning guidelines, a lesson-plan format that can help guide
the teaching of thinking, and a sample lesson plan developed
and taught by a student teacher interested in nurturing the
growth of reflective learners. The chapter concludes with
suggestions for finding sympathetic colleagues to join our
quest to encourage students to think critically.

Setting Goals

When we set out to create a lesson plan, most of us don't start
with clearly stated, measurable objectives in mind. We're
more likely to begin by thinking about the knowledge we

want students to gain or by envisioning a specific classroom activity—even if this sometimes involves little more than keeping chaos at bay. At some stage of the planning process, however, we're likely to establish instructional goals to give purpose to our teaching. Integrating goals for teaching critical thinking into our broader objectives is an important element of this process.

Anyone who reads or attends conferences about critical thinking is bound to encounter references to "higher-order" and "lower-order" thinking. These references often suggest that encouraging higher-order thinking is important and desirable, while encouraging lower-order thinking is less so.

But what are higher- and lower-order thinking? And why is one considered more important and desirable than the other? In fact, these are catch-all terms that derive from Benjamin Bloom's taxonomy of cognitive objectives, a system for ordering instruction developed by Bloom and his colleagues. It became a hierarchy of cognitive objectives that moved from "low" to "high" as follows:

— *Knowledge*—Recalling information.
— *Comprehension*—Translating or interpreting information.
— *Application*—Using knowledge gained to solve problems.
— *Analysis*—Breaking down concepts or ideas to understand the relationship of the parts to the whole.
— *Synthesis*—Putting together something original (e.g., writing an essay).
— *Evaluation*—Judging something against specific criteria.

Advocates of this schema often identify knowledge, comprehension and application as lower-order thinking, and analysis, synthesis and evaluation as higher-order thinking.

Although Bloom's taxonomy is widely known and often helpful, using it as a guide to neatly pigeonhole instructional tasks isn't necessarily as straightforward as it seems. For example, tasks that appear to require only lower-order thinking, such as comprehending a text assigned for reading, may actually require readers to engage in extensive reflection on the author's claims and to apply many strategies that demonstrate critical thought.

Clearly, borrowing from Bloom's taxonomy to suggest that encouraging critical thinking entails little more than introducing tasks that require higher-order thinking is too simplistic. If we are to approach the teaching of critical thinking with the same enthusiasm and rigor with which we expect students to embrace it, our goals must be very specific. The following is a list of goals that have helped me clarify the critical thinking objectives I wish to integrate into my classroom program. Students will be able to:

1. Demonstrate knowledge of the critical thinking process by:
   — Identifying claims made in discourse.
   — Classifying claims (fact, causal, predictive, evaluative, moral, policy and mixed).
   — Separating complex claims into simpler claims.
   — Identifying and clarifying vocabulary that might complicate an argument (e.g., complex terminology, loaded language, etc.).
   — Identifying or constructing possible counter-arguments sympathetically.
   — Evaluating evidence used to support claims and counter-claims.
   — Comparing and assessing arguments and counter-arguments by engaging in a dialectical process.
   — Formulating effective questions to encourage reflection on claims.
   — Identifying relevant and irrelevant evidence.
   — Applying and assessing statistical or probability tests if relevant.
   — Identifying the inner structure of an argument (inductive, deductive, analogical, etc.) and noting the strengths and weakness of reasoning within this structure.
   — Identifying weaknesses in arguments, such as over-generalizations, fallacies of partiality, non sequiturs, red herrings, and appeals to authority or tradition.
   — Recognizing the effects of sarcasm, ridicule and non-verbal signals during argumentative discourse.
   — Identifying assumptions.

— Identifying beliefs that shape an argument or counter-argument and demonstrating awareness of the effects of their own beliefs on their arguments.

2. Demonstrate a disposition to think critically by:
   — Seeking reasons with rational rigor.
   — Imagining alternative solutions and perspectives.
   — Persevering in acquiring and integrating knowledge.
   — Playing with ideas.
   — Planning both personal and school endeavors.
   — Seeking, applying and evaluating the impact of strategies that promote critical thinking.
   — Evaluating the consequences of beliefs, decisions and actions.
   — Monitoring, managing and reflecting on their thinking to acquire self-knowledge and expand productive thinking.

3. Internalize a transformative outlook by:
   — Demonstrating flexibility with respect to the meaning of claims.
   — Demonstrating an understanding of how and why meanings may change.
   — Understanding and illustrating the hermeneutic circle and its explanatory power with respect to interpreting texts.
   — Demonstrating a willingness to modify their position, belief or decision in the face of reasonable evidence.

4. Understand that critical thinking occurs in contexts by:
   — Acknowledging that thinking arises from and is associated with their own schemata.
   — Increasing awareness of their belief system and its effects on thinking.
   — Observing and becoming sensitive to social interactions that shape their knowledge and beliefs.

Helping students achieve all these goals is an ambitious undertaking that may be daunting for teachers who are consciously integrating critical thinking into the curriculum for the first time. As a result, it may be helpful to start by selecting and focusing on only a few, such as identifying claims made in discourse, breaking complex claims into simpler ones, formulating effective questions to encourage reflection on claims, and so on.

A Portfolio Approach to Assessment

At first glance, leaping from a discussion of goals to a discussion of assessment may seem to leave out an important phase of the planning process: the lesson itself.

Setting goals for learning is of little use, however, unless we have a way of measuring students' progress toward achieving them. We need to be able to monitor the effects of our instruction and adjust it to take into account students' needs, interests and abilities as a course unfolds. As a result, assessment is a continuing process that must be integrated into all instruction. Using a portfolio approach can enable us to keep assessment constantly in mind as we design lessons.

WHAT ARE PORTFOLIOS?

A portfolio is a file of documents, such as essays, learning logs, laboratory reports, group projects and homework assignments, created and maintained by individual students as a record of their learning. As a depository for student-created artifacts, it is useful for encouraging analysis and reflection and measuring changes in a student's thinking.

I usually ask the students in my classes to keep two portfolios: a working portfolio and a demonstration portfolio. The working portfolio contains all the material created for a particular course. The demonstration portfolio contains material selected from the working portfolio to demonstrate a particular aspect of learning.

At appropriate points during the semester or school year, the students select items from their working portfolios to include in their demonstration portfolios. This enables me to adjust my teaching to take into account what I learn from assessing their selections.

PORTFOLIO ASSESSMENT AND CRITICAL THINKING

When we want to assess students' progress toward achieving specific critical-thinking goals, we can ask them to sift through the items in their working portfolios and select one or more that demonstrates a specific element of the program. If students in a math or science class were asked to show what they had done to develop a disposition to monitor, manage and reflect on their thinking, for example, they might choose log entries in which they reflected on their thinking while solving math problems or completing a science experiment. In an English class, students might demonstrate their ability to note strengths and weaknesses in reasoning by selecting an analysis of newspaper editorials or letters to the editor.

It's worth noting that the working portfolios may include a wide variety of materials, from scribbled notes on brainstorming sessions to exam papers that reflect a more traditional approach to measuring mastery of material. This provides a broad range of choice when the students are selecting items to include in the demonstration portfolio.

When students are actively involved not only in the selection process but also in working with the teacher to establish the selection criteria, they feel a sense of ownership of and involvement in both the assessment process and their own learning.

The story of Jack, a student in one of my classes, illustrates the usefulness of portfolio assessment. Jack was a bright, athletic 15-year-old in his second year of high school. Like many of his peers, however, his ability to express an organized argument in writing was limited. Through explicit instruction, I intended to help Jack and his classmates learn the skills needed to write a coherent argumentative essay—from stating the thesis to planning the entire argument.

To measure the students' progress, I analyzed two essays they wrote—one before instruction and one after. In addition, I looked at their notes, outlines and a thinking-aloud protocol I had developed.

When composing the first essay, Jack struggled to find a thesis. He tried to write his thesis before exploring either the essay topic or examining his own knowledge of it. Then, he decided to write out some of his thoughts, but got lost. In his own words, the ideas became "all jumbled up." Finally, he decided to create an outline, which enabled him to organize his thoughts well enough to put together something to hand in. Unfortunately, the argument he developed lacked consistent support and a well-developed counter-argument.

Two months later, Jack wrote another essay on a similar topic. Using strategies we had discussed in class, he quickly formulated a thesis, developed an antithesis, and listed several reasons for supporting both his thesis and antithesis. As his essay unfolded, Jack used the points he had developed to support his thesis as organizing ideas for each paragraph. He also developed a counter-argument using his early notes. Unlike his earlier effort, this paper developed a coherent, persuasive argument, based on a clearly stated, well-supported thesis.

When asked to include a written reflection on the development of his ability to think critically in his demonstration portfolio, Jack compared the process of writing these two essays. In writing the second essay, he identified and constructed probable counter-arguments, compared and assessed arguments and counter-arguments, and identified relevant and irrelevant evidence. He sought, applied and evaluated the impact of strategies that promote critical thinking. In using his own previous knowledge to develop points supporting his thesis and antithesis, he also demonstrated his growing understanding that thinking arises from and is associated with his own schemata.

To measure our students' progress, we can develop scoring guides or benchmarks that indicate stages of mastery of specific critical thinking skills. For example, if the goal is for students to be able to identify various types of claims, the benchmarks might look like this:

— *Beginning*: Students can define the concept of claim and provide an example from their reading.
— *Intermediate*: Students can identify and explain the difference between fact and evaluative claims and provide examples of each.
— *Advanced*: Students can identify, explain and illustrate fact, causal, predictive and evaluative claims.
— *Mastery*: Students can teach others how to identify and illustrate claims of all types.

Developing and using benchmarks like these takes a lot of work. When a critical-thinking program is well-advanced, however, and teachers believe that more rigorous performance-based assessment is likely to yield helpful information, the effort required to do so may be worthwhile.

Planning Lessons That Integrate Critical Thinking

When writing lesson plans, most of us follow a tried-and-true structure that includes features such as learning objectives, materials, warm-up, teaching method (e.g., direct instruction, lecture-discussion, discovery, and so on), and methods of evaluation. We can, of course, vary this structure by adding features that encourage us to reflect on what we are doing and why. The suggested format looks like this:

Lesson Plan

Lesson (with key descriptive words):

Class: Date:

Objectives (with reasons for identifying):

Objective for Thinking (with reasons for identifying):

Connection between Objectives and Broader Goals for Unit or Semester:

Materials (with reasons for selecting):

Procedures (including approximate time allowed):

   Focusing Activity (with reasons for selecting):

   Introduction (with tie to previous learning):

   Lesson Structure (e.g., presentation with modeling and practice, inquiry project, lecture-discussion, etc., with reasons for selecting):

   Method(s) of Evaluation (with reasons for selecting):

   Homework Assignment(s) (with reasons for selecting):

Expected Student Response to Lesson (with reasons for expectation):

Reflections (after lesson):

This format can encourage us to justify our decision to include each element of a lesson and, once the lesson is over, reflect in writing on what worked, what didn't, what we might modify the next time we teach the lesson, and what we discovered or noticed about ourselves and our students during the lesson. We can always, even the most experienced among us, benefit from examining our instructional decisions and monitoring the effectiveness of our teaching strategies.

A student teacher in one of my classes, Cathy Lee was practice teaching in an economics class in a large Los Angeles high school. In one of her reflective papers, she wrote, "During the start of my student teaching, I had set some expectations. Some were high and some were low. I had this ideal picture in my mind of affecting most of the students' learning; however, I quickly discovered that I was not going to reach every single student, though a handful were reachable."

Early in her experience with the economics class, she recognized that too few students were participating in discussions. So, with the assistance of her master teacher, she began to develop lessons designed to "stress the application of what the students' learned, as well as draw out their creativity." In doing this, she was creating an environment that encouraged critical thinking.

One day, I observed Lee teach a lesson that she had designed as part of a larger unit on consumer economics. Although her objective for the lesson stated, "Students will be able to decide whether it is more economical to purchase a store brand or a name brand," Lee's purposes were broader and deeper than this. By engaging students in a controlled evaluation of common foods, such as colas and popcorns, she hoped to develop their awareness of differences in nutritional value, taste and price, to decide which products they preferred, and to encourage them to think about their reasons for preferring one product over another.

Though some might fault the selection of colas and popcorn as the foods to be evaluated, a lesson like this is tailor-made for encouraging critical thinking. It engages students in at least two so-called higher-order forms of thinking: analysis and evaluation. And the evaluation encourages them to reflect rationally on claims about what to believe and what to do. It also involves them in identifying claims, examining evidence, discovering more about their own thinking processes, and comparing and assessing arguments and counter-arguments.

Lee gathered large bottles of three different colas, including a store brand, and three kinds of popcorn, already popped. One of these was also a store brand. All the brand names were hidden. Also on hand were paper cups, a couple of bowls, and some paper napkins.

Lee began by asking questions that encouraged the students to focus on the forthcoming activity: Why do you buy particular soft drinks and snacks? To what extent do brand names influence your selection of products? If you were going to have a party, what brand of cola and popcorn would you probably buy?

These questions sparked a brief discussion about the influence of advertising on consumers and enabled Lee to tie the lesson to the unit on budgeting included in the students' textbook. She then distributed an information sheet outlining the ingredients of the various brands of cola and popcorn, as well as their cost.

Next, Lee recruited several students to help distribute samples of the products so the class could conduct the taste tests. She then asked the following questions and recorded the students' responses on the chalkboard: What did each cola (popcorn) taste like? Which did you prefer and why? What criteria are most important to you?

In addition to helping students focus on the specific objectives of the economics elements of the lesson, these questions encouraged them to think critically by asking them not only to give reasons for their preferences but also to think about their standards for judging quality.

Although most of the students tended to favor the widely known brand-name colas and popcorns, several said they preferred the less well-known store brands. Once they learned which price went with which taste, however, some students realized they could get more cola or popcorn for less money and indicated that they would be inclined to sacrifice a little taste for a greater quantity.

Unlike the earlier lessons in which they had been reluctant to engage in discussion, the students participated enthusiastically in this activity. They all wanted to express their opinions and responded eagerly when Lee prodded them to back these up. They said things like, "This cola's too sweet," "This cola tastes flat," "This cola has a zip to it," "This popcorn's not salty enough," and "The butter doesn't taste right on this popcorn." In a highly concrete way, Lee was encouraging them to back up their evaluative claims with reasons based on personal taste preferences.

The class also discussed how decisions about grocery purchases are made and how a family's food budget is allocated. Students talked about the influence of marketing techniques on their buying habits and about marketing campaigns, such as those for cigarettes, beer, clothes and cosmetics.

In fact, the students had so much to say that they were still talking about product pitches as they were leaving the classroom after the bell rang. On the way out, one student asked, "Did we just have a party or a class?"

Although Lee's lesson was certainly a great success, time limitations prevented her from expanding the discussion to encourage the students to explore both the function of standards in their decisions and how these standards can help them make other judgments of value or worth. With a little more time, she might, for example, have introduced product evaluations published in magazines like *Consumer Reports*.

Lee might also have improved the lesson by redesigning the homework assignment, which asked students to complete a reading from the course textbook. Unfortunately, this assignment wasn't strongly related to the lesson she had presented. A different activity might have encouraged the students to explore more fully some of their observations about product quality and marketing. Had students kept learning logs, for example, they might have written personal responses to the activity, shared them the next day in small groups or with the whole class, and then worked them into a consumer report.

Despite its relatively minor limitations, however, this economics lesson provided the students with many opportunities to think critically as they reflected on claims made in the consumer marketplace.

At the end of her practice teaching session, Lee reflected in writing on the planning process: "When I reflect on my daily lesson plans, I feel that I have grown a lot. It was a challenge to try new lessons. I was not sure if they were going to work, but shortly I discovered that it did not matter if they worked or not because I would learn from the experience...I believe that the key to effective lessons is to spend time planning things out thoroughly and making careful assessments after you try the lesson."

The Role of Critical Friends

When beginning to design lessons that integrate critical thinking, a little help from our friends is worthwhile. This help can come from what Arthur Costa calls a critical friend—a person who, like an optometrist, helps us see more clearly what's going on in our planning and teaching.

In addition to acting as a sounding board as we explain our purposes for teaching critical thinking, this friend can comment on our plans, observe our teaching, and provide feedback that helps bring our work into focus. Finding a person to do this is not easy, however. Over the years, I've found that few of us have such a person in our professional lives.

Yet I've reaped many benefits from collaborating with critical friends. Though I have certainly given away lots of ideas, I've also gotten lots back. The perspective of my critical friends has helped me see things that needed to be reworked. In the process, we all grew as reflective teachers of reflective learners.

Conclusion

The approaches to planning explored in this chapter help us think through the design of our instruction in thinking and reflect on our teaching, perhaps with the help of a supportive colleague. With the groundwork laid for thoughtful teaching, the following chapters will examine activities, strategies and procedures that can contribute to the development of thinking through talking, reading and writing.

. . . .

THINKING

THROUGH TALKING

Often, to talk is to discover what we think. For example, the teachers whose story was told in the introduction knew little about their own and their colleagues' views on the teaching of thinking until they began talking about it. Their conversation—the questions they asked one another and the answers they gave—revealed their thinking and clarified the issues they needed to grapple with. Yet people often take the view that critical thinking begins with reading and writing when it actually begins, for most of us, with talk.

Language and Thought

Although Jean Piaget and Bärbel Inhelder wrote in 1969 that "language does not constitute the source of logic but is, on the contrary, structured by it," Lev Vygotsky believed the opposite: that language drives, rather than follows, cognitive development. From a Vygotskian perspective, language mediates our thinking and enables us to move to "higher ground." In other words, language has the power to shape what—and how—we think.

When we think, we typically talk silently to ourselves in a register that Vygotsky called inner speech. Some of us even talk aloud to ourselves from time to time. Of course, we also talk to others. In our conversations with ourselves, we may reflect on what others have said to us; in speaking with others, however, we may express aloud what we've said to ourselves.

Conversation—with ourselves and others—provides fertile ground for the growth of thinking. In the talk between parent and child, the seeds for learning how to think and how to think about thinking are sown. When formal schooling begins, teachers provide further opportunities for children to develop their thinking skills. The talk that goes on in the classroom provides children with both the opportunity to construct new knowledge and the strategies to make this knowledge useful. As schooling progresses, learners acquire and extend knowledge of many different kinds: general knowledge about the world and domain-specific knowledge about subjects such as history, biology and mathematics. While acquiring declarative knowledge, or knowledge of *what*, they also gain information about *how* to do things, which is sometimes called procedural or strategic knowledge. And as they learn *when* and *why* to use both their declarative and procedural knowledge, they develop conditional knowledge.

The notion that we learn to think by talking was firmly appreciated long ago. In his dialogues, Socrates tried to teach his friends to think by engaging them in discussions that established comparisons, analyzed meanings, spotted weaknesses in arguments, probed for clarification, built counter-arguments and so on. In fact, he was so convinced of the power of dialogue to develop thoughtfulness and discover truth that he appeared to be rather skeptical of the contribution of reading and writing to the development of thinking.

Teachers who understand the importance of talk in developing reflective learners try to establish and sustain a classroom environment that encourages conversation. Vygotsky described how interactions using language enhance mental growth. When teachers use language in a way that enables students to know or do something independently that they previously did not know or could not do on their own, they have helped them interact in what Vygotsky called their zone of proximal development. This is the region that exists between what learners can do on their own and what they can do with the help of a more able person, such as a teacher or more knowledgeable peer.

In *Thought and Language*, Vygotsky wrote that the best instruction is directed "not so much at the ripe as at the ripening functions." To help students become independent, reflective learners, teachers need to determine their zone of proximal development and use conversation to enable them to do alone tomorrow what they can do today only with the help of others. Many teachers have found that carefully designed cooperative learning activities are an ideal vehicle for providing students with opportunities to do this.

But Talk about What?

If talk is essential to developing the ability to think, what kind of talk does this most effectively? Although programs that promote critical thinking can take many forms, I usually focus first on argumentation, the study of arguments.

Arguments are often intricate webs of meaning spun in talk. By looking closely at how these webs of meaning, often designed in fear or fury, hold together, students can learn much about themselves, their thinking and the power of language.

Before I unload my reasons for studying arguments on the students, however, I encourage them to come up with their own reasons. The more they produce, the better. When students develop reasons for learning that are meaningful to them, it improves their motivation, as well as their sense of purpose and ownership of the curriculum.

To set the stage, I often begin by asking students to take 10 minutes or so to reflect in writing on the question, Why study arguments? These reflections lay the groundwork for a session in which they work in small groups to talk about the reasons they have come up with and share them with the class.

If necessary, I flesh out this discussion with reasons they may have overlooked. These are often drawn from the material presented at the beginning of the previous chapter. To focus students' attention and help guide our investigation, I often present questions such as the following:

— What is an argument?
— Why and how do people argue in day-to-day life?
— What kinds of things do people argue about?
— What mental moves do people make when they argue?
— Where did they learn those moves?
— Of the people you know, who does best in arguments? What do these individuals do to conduct successful arguments?

— What do you observe other people doing when they argue on TV, in movies, on radio talk-shows, around campus, in their families, or in a conflict with friends?
— How are arguments or disputes orchestrated or controlled in public places like courtrooms or municipal council chambers?

It's worth noting that students aren't the only ones who learn from investigating arguments. As teachers, we can explore answers to the same questions—and others that are likely to help us improve our teaching of critical thinking. Some of these other questions are:

— What kinds of skills can we, as teachers, develop and model to help students understand and negotiate arguments more effectively?
— How can we help students learn about tactics and emotions during arguments while role-playing, improvising, acting out scenes from plays, or doing courtroom simulations?
— What kinds of questions help us encourage students to be reflective listeners in dialogue?
— How can we teach students to formulate and ask questions that help them understand issues more thoroughly?
— What can we do to engender more and better talk in the classroom? Are the principles that guide good arguments in print the same as those that guide conversational arguments?

Although talk is the primary mode for developing socially constructed knowledge and critical thinking in schools, this talk is most effective when it's integrated with reading and writing. As a result, this chapter will focus on talk, and those that follow will deal with reading and writing.

Talking Arguments

Because one of my aims is to encourage students to argue more effectively by reflecting on how they've handled arguments in the past, I try to draw on their own experiences to help us define what argument is and discover the rational and emotional strategies people use when they argue. How do students weave the webs of argument? How do they try to "win" arguments? How do they present their position—get their "truth" out?

To get students talking as soon as possible, I begin by asking them to think about arguments they have been involved in. For most teenagers, these arguments are with parents, friends or teachers and are often sparked by conflicts over their efforts to establish their independence and sense of identity.

I might introduce this activity by asking students to describe one of their "best" arguments in a journal, log or letter to me. To ensure that they don't feel that their privacy is being invaded, I emphasize that they can select *one* of their best—it doesn't have to be *the* best.

Students don't usually ask me to define what I mean by an argument; rather, they seem to use their folk knowledge of the subject. Nevertheless, in case someone asks, I have a simple definition ready so they know what they need to remember and think about. I explain that an argument is a dispute or conflict with another person that usually involves a difference of opinion, though it can also involve trying to persuade someone of something or being persuaded of something. The dispute is usually verbal, but it may even be physical.

Once the students have had time to write their descriptions, I invite them to share their stories with the class or, if they aren't ready to do this right away, in small groups.

As the students talk, I gently prod them to fill in details by asking questions about what set off the argument, how they felt at certain stages, how others might have been feeling, and what the participants said and did. As students tell their stories, I encourage the others to listen carefully, take notes and watch for strategies used by the participants, such as pointing out contradictions, doing something they know will irritate and annoy the adversary, or moving in "for the kill" when a weakness is noticed.

We then review the argument and, on the chalkboard, I jot down the features that prompted them to choose it as one of the best. These features usually focus on the issues that sparked the dispute and the strategies used by the participants. We follow up with a discussion of these features.

We then do the same with their "worst" arguments, which students typically describe as arguments they've "lost."

This activity, which gives us a list of themes, strategies and patterns for arguments, often stretches over a couple of classes. It's important to be flexible about the time allotted, adjusting the schedule to take into account students' interest and other curricular demands. In fact, the students' enthusiasm usually generates a great deal of discussion and excitement. When listening, they are often eager to ask questions to clarify who said what to whom and what the outcomes were. When talking about their best arguments, they frequently express pride in what they said and the way they said it. Although this pride is usually less evident when they describe their worst arguments, other features, such as I-really-should-have-said scenarios, often emerge.

LANGUAGE FUNCTIONS DURING ARGUMENTS

As chief information manager and guide for this activity, teachers can help students make sense of the patterns that occur in these arguments by encouraging them to reflect on the arguments and distill what was happening—sometimes beneath the words.

Getting beneath the words is the aspect of this activity that I enjoy most. I've found that learning about the ways the students and I use language has helped me understand them—and my interactions with them—better.

Pragmatics, the study of the way utterances are interpreted in a social context, involves examining what a speaker means rather than what she says. For example, someone who says, "I'm cold," may actually mean, "I want you to close that window."

The following dialogue between an imaginary teenager named Carol and her mother is typical of the arguments recounted by students. Although the information in square brackets identifies a function of each utterance, this isn't definitive. Furthermore, there is little commentary on intonation, although, as we know, the way something is said makes all the difference!

Mother: Where did you go last night? [Questioning]
Carol: To Sally's to watch a video. [Giving information]
Mother: No you didn't. [Challenging]

Carol: Jennifer was there, too. She'll tell you I was there with them both. [Giving counter-evidence]

Mother: Oh really? Matt said he saw you down at Jack-in-the-Box last night. [Repudiating evidence]

Carol: Where I was is none of your business.[Challenging]

Mother: What time did you leave Sally's? [Requesting clarification]

Carol: Jennifer's brother came to pick her up at nine o'clock. Ask him if you don't believe me or Jennifer. [Confirming evidence]

Mother: I wouldn't trust that knucklehead to tell me the right time of day. [Insulting, repudiating status of evidence]

Carol: He's no knucklehead. [Denying]

Mother: Well, Sally's is off limits for you from now on. [Establishing domination]

Carol: (mockingly) Sally's is off limits from now on.[Using mockery to challenge]

Mother: Don't you sass me! [Establishing domination]

Carol: This is the fourth time this month you've told me I can't see my friends. [Listing disagreements]

Mother: It's only the second time. [Challenging]

Carol: Fourth.

Mother: Second.

Carol: Fourth.

Mother: Second!

Carol gets up and walks out of the room. [Withdrawing]

Because identifying what is really going on as an argument progresses enhances understanding, asking students to write out and analyze a dialogue in this way is a good idea. Students can do this in small groups, then share their analysis with the rest of the class.

As they observe and discuss argumentative discourse, students expand the list of verbal and non-verbal strategies used by participants to accomplish their goals. As in the argument between Carol and her mother, these strategies often shift attention away from the issue that sparked the dispute to focus on the individuals involved.

LEARNING-LOG FOLLOW-UP

Although I find that talking our way into critical thinking is an excellent approach, I also try to encourage students to write

46

about this talk as soon as possible. As a follow-up to talk-centered activities, I suggest that they write about what they have learned about arguing as a result of discussing their own arguments and those of their classmates. What have they learned about themselves as arguers? This reflection may, of course, spark further discussion.

THE BIG THREE

To focus on the emotional impact of arguments rather than on their success or failure, an alternative approach is to ask students to talk about three of their "biggest" arguments—those that were the most upsetting or disturbing. Again, I emphasize that they need not write about arguments they don't want to disclose and that they won't be pressured to talk about arguments they want to keep to themselves.

I begin by asking students to write brief descriptions of three of their biggest arguments. If they request an example, I choose one from my own experience or one that another student has used in the past. To help them focus, I suggest that they consider questions like the following:

— What led to the argument?
— What was the argument about?
— Why were you involved in it?
— What was the setting?
— What was at stake for you?
— How was the argument conducted?
— What were some of the strategies used to persuade others to accept a particular point of view?
— Who won? Who lost? How do you know?
— If you could run an instant replay of the argument, what, if anything, would you say or do differently?

Once students have finished writing, I guide the class through much the same kind of discussion and follow-up as described in the previous activity. Again, discussion is often animated and the teacher's role is to moderate, encourage and record information.

INNERVIEW

This activity helps students share and build metacognitive knowledge about their ability to monitor, assess and manage their performance in an argument. They work in pairs to interview each other to discover how they view themselves when arguing and what they know about themselves as arguers. The following questions help guide the interview:

— Do you consider yourself good at arguing, or poor or somewhere in between? Why do you rate yourself this way?

— Have people every commented on your arguing style or behavior? If so, what did they say? Do you agree or disagree with their comments? Why?

— Do you like or dislike arguing? Why?

— Do you try to avoid arguments? If so, why? If not, why not? If you do try to avoid them, what tactics do you use?

— What strategies do you usually use in arguments? Or what are some of the things you've said or done when you were in arguments?

— Do you think your ability to argue has improved over the years? If so, why? If not, why not?

— Do any of your friends argue with you? If so, what do you argue about and how do your arguments usually proceed and end?

— Did you learn how to argue from anyone? If so, whom? What did you learn?

— If someone were to ask you what makes a good arguer, what would you say? What would you say makes a poor arguer?

— If someone were to ask your advice on how to improve his ability to argue, what would you say?

I use various strategies to encourage students to talk about what they discovered about themselves and their partners during the interviews. For example, I might ask the partners to present each other's responses to a particular question. Sometimes, I suggest that each pair select the question they want to report; at other times, I select a question and ask one student to answer as her partner might.

Another approach involves adapting the innerview questions to create a classroom survey. This can be as simple as asking the students to respond to a question with a show of hands, then counting the responses and recording them on the chalkboard.

This activity can also be an effective springboard to creating mini-biographies or thumbnail sketches. Students can draw on the information they have gathered about their partner to write a profile focusing on their partner's history with respect to arguments. This gives them a chance to transform what they have discovered into a coherent biographical sketch that emphasizes one aspect of a person's life.

The activity also provides me with an opportunity to collect a great deal of information about students' attitudes toward and knowledge of argumentation. Because many students have given this area of their lives little thought, it's important to provide them with a chance to learn some important and interesting things about themselves and their peers. For teachers, too, this is an opportunity to learn about the students.

How Others Deal with Arguments

Once students have talked about arguments and examined their own arguing styles, it's time to shift the emphasis to argument strategies used by other people. These may include friends and relatives, people in business and the professions, and people on radio and television.

FRIENDS AND RELATIVES

To follow up the investigation of students' experiences with and attitudes toward arguments, I suggest casting the net wider by gathering more information about arguments and their structure. The purpose is to discover more about the students' history and behavior when dealing with conflicts and issues.

Interviewing friends and relatives to discover prevalent, preferred and proscribed strategies and patterns of argument is an effective way of doing this. To help guide their interviews, I work with the students to come up with a list of questions they can use. These questions are often similar to the following:

— What are the attitudes of friends and relatives toward arguing?
— Are any behaviors discouraged or forbidden among friends or relatives during arguments?

— What are considered the best ways of handling differences of opinion when they arise between friends or within families?
— Who is considered the most effective arguer in your friendship or family circle? Why?

GOVERNMENT, BUSINESS AND THE PROFESSIONS

Working in teams, students can visit municipal councilors, members of the clergy, businesspeople, lawyers, journalists, doctors, insurance adjusters, school administrators and others to gather information about the way arguments are conducted in public discourse. Again, I work with the students to put together lists of questions to help guide the interviews. These lists often look like this:

— What have you learned about arguments in your work and in public life?
— Is there something that stands out as the most important thing you've learned about arguing?
— What have you come to admire in arguments? What do you detest in arguments?
— How do you usually go about arguing?
— What advice would you give young people about verbal conflicts and argumentation?

If students discover community members who are particularly good at talking persuasively, these individuals might be invited to class to discuss the role of argument in public discourse and democracy.

RADIO AND TELEVISION

Students are probably familiar with a variety of radio and television programs, both local and national, that focus on issues ranging from the serious to the sensational. In many cases, the hosts of these shows—Oprah Winfrey, Geraldo Rivera and so on—are household names.

These broadcasts provide a rich resource that can help expand students' awareness of argumentative discourse. For example, teachers can tape various programs for students to view in class. Be careful, however, to check and adhere to laws governing the taping of copyrighted material.

Invite students to observe, take notes on, analyze and discuss how the hosts move through the program. Some of them are adept at bringing guests and audiences into confrontations, but how productive are these? What do their goals appear to be? Do the hosts seek consensus and resolution, or strive for more heat than light? What seems to emerge from the encounters?

As an alternative, ask pairs or small groups of students to monitor a particular show, tape appropriate sections, and present their findings to the class. Questions such as the following can help guide this inquiry:

— What kinds of issues are presented?
— How are the issues presented to the audience?
— How do talk-show hosts use language to control the presentation of different sides of an issue or problem and how do they control the building of arguments?
— What strategies do talk-show hosts use during interviews or encounters between guests?
— What do participants appear to learn during the programs?
— What does the audience appear to get from the discussions?

Students can learn much by listening to and watching these programs, especially if they have an opportunity to compare the topics and arguing styles. Because they may be tempted to focus on the issues presented, it's important to remind them that this isn't as important as examining the process used to present them.

Enacting Arguments

Watching and participating in re-enactments of arguments helps students learn more about arguing styles and strategies. These enactments may be highly structured and controlled, as in the case of scripted plays, or less structured and far less controlled, as in the case of improvised role-playing.

DRAMA

Whether a play is written by Sophocles or Neil Simon, it would be hard to find one that doesn't turn on conflicts that emerge as arguments between characters. Although many plays contain examples of argument, two of the most engaging for adolescents are *Twelve Angry Men*, the story of how one skeptic affected a jury's decision on the fate of a young man, and *Inherit the Wind*, the story of the Scopes trial in the United States in which a teacher was charged with presenting the arguments for evolution. Reading, acting and discussing plays or even parts of plays such as these provides students with many opportunities to study effective argument strategies and to take a role—a safe role—in developing arguments.

One worthwhile avenue of discussion involves comparing courtroom arguments, which are controlled by a complex set of rules and regulations, with arguments that take place outside court. Students can be encouraged to consider which courtroom procedures, if any, might be transferred to everyday life to make social disputes more manageable.

SIMULATIONS

Simulations, which provide students with an opportunity to role-play famous—or infamous—historical characters in a form of controlled argument, are an engaging way both to build knowledge and to gain thinking skills.

Creating simulations also provides an excellent opportunity for teachers in various departments to work together to integrate the curriculum. Simulated debates between key figures might spring from issues such as the following:

— The form of constitution in a new democracy.
— The British ambivalence over declaring war on Germany as other European countries were being invaded in the late 1930s.
— The abolition of slavery or the Civil War in the United States.
— The unionization of labor.
— Liberal versus conservative approaches to economic development and control.
— The construction and use of the atomic bomb at the end of World War II.
— The entry of the United States into the Vietnam War.
— The proposed separation of Quebec from Canada.
— The role of Western countries in the decline of the former Soviet Union.

— The wisdom of controlling the world's population.

Because of the research involved, simulations are often time-consuming to prepare. Fortunately, a variety of simulations is available commercially. These include simulated trials, legislative battles and critical debates over momentous policy issues.

DEBATES

Taking sides on issues that are important to them and their communities gives students a chance to practice argument techniques and get feedback on their effectiveness. Debates also offer teachers opportunities to observe students in the debate context and to gather more information about how students' minds work in a social confrontation, albeit one that is controlled.

Although debates can be organized in many different ways, I have found that two formats work particularly well. The first is a variation of the traditional formal debate structure; the second involves the whole class.

Traditional Debate

This classical approach involves establishing specific resolutions to be debated, such as, Resolved: Cigarettes will be classified as a controlled substance and regulated by the government. Teachers can select resolutions to fit the needs of the curriculum, or the class can help select and draft them.

In small groups, students prepare arguments for and against the resolution. To encourage the teams to be prepared to argue either side of a question, I don't usually tell them in advance which position they will take. As a resource person, I try to provide information—more or less equal in quantity and quality—about each side so that teams can develop their positions. Students may also need guidance and time to find additional materials. A key part of the preparation process involves ensuring that they are able to make their arguments in the time allotted for each stage of the debate.

When the teams are ready or the preparation time is up, team captains flip a coin to decide which side they take. The team arguing in favor of the resolution begins. The opposing team refutes this argument, then presents its own argument against the resolution. The team for the resolution then has an opportunity to refute the argument of the opposition. Finally, both sides summarize their positions and conclude. Part of the challenge for the teams is to express their arguments coherently in the time allotted.

The performance of the two teams can be evaluated by the entire class or by a smaller group of students. In both cases, I find that a rating sheet helps them assess important features, such as the quantity and quality of evidence, the coherence and clarity of arguments, the validity of points made during rebuttal, the persuasiveness of the presenters, and overall impression. I usually design the evaluation sheet to show a score for each feature, as well as an overall score.

Whole-Class Debate

Less formal than traditional debates, this format works best when student opinion on an issue is more or less evenly split. A survey can reveal what some of these issues are. The issue can then be phrased in the form of a resolution or question (e.g., Should grades be abolished?), and background can be discussed.

I invite the students to decide which team they want to join and organize the teams on opposite sides of the classroom. Teams don't need to be the same size. Each appoints a captain and a coin-toss determines which side begins. A member of the beginning team opens argument, then a member of the opposing team responds and presents an opposing position. Taking turns, the teams go back and forth until all arguments have been voiced. Some teachers even encourage students who are persuaded by the opposing team's arguments to change sides, a practice that adds excitement to the activity.

To encourage the students to control the speaking order, a large ball is a good gatekeeping measure. Only the student holding the ball can speak and, once finished speaking, she or he must pass it to a speaker on the other team. It also helps to establish guidelines designed to discourage one person on a team from monopolizing possession of the ball.

Because students can move between teams, I don't usually evaluate these debates formally. If a winner must be declared, the number of bodies on a team is an immediate visual evaluation of which team's arguments were most convincing.

Follow-Up

No matter which debate format is chosen, the follow-up is very important. I like to give students time to debrief—engage in a kind of post-debate meta-talk about the talking that was done. These questions can help guide this discussion:

— What kinds of things, with respect to content, did students say that were persuasive?
— Were there ways in which students presented their ideas that worked particularly well?
— What improvements in strategy would you suggest?

I also like to provide time for students to write about the debate. This may involve evaluating how it went from their personal perspective, what they learned from it, or whether they changed their view on the issue—and why.

IMPROVISED ROLE-PLAYING

Improvised role-playing provides a less controlled format for presenting arguments. Although this format certainly gives students an opportunity to experiment in an atmosphere of freedom and spontaneity, it requires careful planning by the teacher. Viola Spolin's classic *Improvisation for the Theatre* or Patrick Verriour's *In Role: Teaching and Learning Dramatically* are excellent resources.

Topics

When choosing a topic, it's important to keep in mind the students' abilities, their level of self-control, the sensitivity of particular students to certain issues, and their general readiness to participate in and watch role-playing. Remember that, once a role-play is under way, the teacher can't always control its direction or what individuals say. Whether this form of role-playing is appropriate for a particular class is something every teacher needs to assess carefully.

The topics can range from a radio talk-show on teenage dating to differences of opinion between friends, between a teacher and student, or even between a student and parents. Variations such as these give students a chance to play the role of an authority figure who must deal with a conflict and decide what seems best for all concerned.

Structure

When planning an improvised role-play, it's important to clearly identify and design the situation, the participants, the setting and the problem. Start small and provide plenty of structure; for example, a first effort might begin with two students role-playing a telephone conversation about a conflict caused when one of them offended the other.

Once everyone is familiar with the process and expectations, the scenarios can become more ambitious and involve more students.

GROUP INQUIRY PROJECTS

Inquiry projects are structured investigations. Using the scientific method, the intent of the inquiry is to gather evidence to support, reject or modify a claim. For example, an inquiry might be designed to evaluate the claim that nothing burns without oxygen. Science classes usually bristle with inquiry projects.

One talented teacher became known as the Toilet Queen of Davenport, Iowa, because of an inquiry project. It started with a problem: a clogged toilet in the home of a student who reported that toilet paper had caused the problem. Joan McShane and the 11- and 12-year-olds in her class decided to find out why toilet paper clogs toilets and which brand of paper is best from an ecological and practical point of view.

To conduct the investigation, McShane and a parent designed a special toilet so the class could run tests on 43 brands of toilet paper to see which broke up best and retained the least water. Community members, including sewage treatment experts, engineers, ecologists and paper company representatives, visited the class to talk about toilet paper and its disposal. This inquiry project convinced the students that science can help them solve many of life's daily problems.

Inquiry projects need not be limited to science classes, however. They can be used in all disciplines to teach students how to structure an inquiry, and how to gather and apply evidence to test the validity of claims.

Furthermore, inquiry projects can be designed so that teacher and students use talk to shape and guide the inquiry, whether this is as a whole class or in small groups. The consumer economics project described in the previous chapter is an example of an inquiry project involving a whole class.

One of the most effective small-group inquiry projects I've seen was designed by Gary Okey, a former lawyer who was practice teaching in a history class in the San Francisco Bay area. He asked the 16- and 17-year-old students to draw on their knowledge of the American Constitution, its amendments, and other legal precedents to conduct a "judicial review" of various statutes. Because the laws Okey selected had actually been reviewed by the Supreme Court, the students were able to compare their decisions with those of the Supreme Court justices.

Okey divided the class into eight small groups. Two groups worked on one of the four laws being reviewed. One argued for upholding a law; the other argued for its repeal. To complete the assignment, students needed to be able to understand the law under review and cite principles from the Constitution or other legal precedents to support their arguments.

This project was an exemplary lesson in thinking. Each team was required to find evidence in existing documents, apply this evidence and, in a report to the whole class, convince other students of the correctness of their position. Furthermore, as they were preparing to present their case to the class, students had to talk and argue extensively and persuasively with each other.

Once a pair of teams had made their presentations, the rest of the class played the role of the judges, voting on which presentation was most persuasive.

Fostering Thinking through Questioning and Discussion

There is no question that a teacher's ability to question artfully and guide discussions effectively enhances the development of thinking through talk. Books such as Francis Hunkins' *Teaching Thinking through Effective Questioning* provide both material and strategies that can be used to create a questioning classroom environment.

THINKING ABOUT QUESTIONS

Researchers such as Hugh Mehan have found that teachers' questions often follow a pattern. The ritual begins when a teacher asks a question such as, "When was the Battle of Hastings?" When a student responds with the correct answer—"1066"—the teacher evaluates this response: "That's right. Very good." While this kind of initiate-respond-evaluate pattern can aid instruction in some cases, it occurs too often in too many classrooms.

Furthermore, in many classrooms, teachers tend to guide and control most of the questioning. Classrooms in which students are given a high degree of responsibility for framing topics for discussion and for conducting conversations about those topics among themselves are few and far between.

Yet, teachers know that asking questions that activate metacognition and require the deep processing of knowledge results in more efficient learning. We also know that it's more effective to ask questions throughout a discussion or lesson rather than to concentrate them at a single point. Undoubtedly, this result is related to the activation of background knowledge and its processing and change.

We also know that the kind of question asked is likely to influence the kind of learning acquired. If we want students to become more reflective, we need to ask—and encourage the students to ask one another—questions that require them to engage in analysis, problem-solving and inquiry.

Furthermore, to get the most from students when asking questions, it's important to phrase questions clearly, to give them time to think, to keep them engaged and focused during dialogue, to encourage them to listen to their own answers, to probe answers for the sake of clarification, and to respond constructively.

Because asking effective questions is so important to developing critical thinking, we must understand the process and look for ways to develop the art of questioning in both ourselves and the students.

Monitoring the effectiveness of our own questions is the first step in this process. Although teachers can prepare many questions ahead of time, we also need to be able to pose spontaneous questions as discussion proceeds. Audio- or videotaping classroom discussions enables us to observe our performance and assess our questioning techniques and take steps to improve them.

It also helps to find a supportive colleague who is willing to observe live instruction or, if this isn't possible, to watch a videotape to identify what worked, what didn't, and what could have been improved.

Teachers can help students develop their questioning skills by serving as a model and ensuring that they have opportunities to practice. One strategy that does this is ReQuest, developed by Anthony Manzo. By encouraging students to ask questions of the teacher after reading a section of an argument, ReQuest reverses the typical pattern in which the teacher asks questions, often from a prepared list, to which the answers are already known.

At first, the students' questions tend to be similar to those they're used to hearing from teachers. After fielding the students' questions, I ask mine, which are designed to elicit reasoned reflection about claims made, evidence given, counter-arguments that might be developed, and weaknesses in the argument. After reading another section of text, we repeat the process. As we continue, students begin to pick up on the kinds of questions I'm asking and their own questions become more probing.

Students usually enjoy ReQuest, not only because it puts the teacher on the spot—I better make sure I've done my homework!—but also because it enables them to get answers to their own questions. In addition, using ReQuest encourages students to carry the ball during classroom conversations rather than relying on the teacher to initiate the interactions.

Another question-generating strategy that works well is one I learned from the Bay Area Writing Project, a group of San Francisco area educators who meet periodically at the University of California, Berkeley, to exchange approaches that improve literacy and learning. Once students have finished a reading, I ask them to record all the questions they can about it. Although the main purpose of this activity is to open minds to questions—to foster a skeptical spirit—rather than give answers, the students often read their questions to one another in small groups to and answer as many as possible.

PREPARING FOR DISCUSSIONS

Effective discussions don't just happen. The groundwork needs to be laid carefully.

Because effective communication among students is essential to a successful discussion, the environment needs to be conducive to group interaction. When desks are in rows, participants can't always see each other clearly. Although I've found that a circle or U-shaped seating pattern works best, I've also participated in many productive discussions in classrooms with the desks in rows because the climate for inquiry was right.

Teachers also need to be thoroughly familiar with the material to be discussed. The more we know about the subject of discussion, whether it's cell division, Roman history, or *Romeo and Juliet*, the more opportunities we'll have to contribute knowledge, and clarify and guide questioning. Confidence and personal comfort also ride higher when we're knowledgeable and well-prepared.

Investing time in preparing an outline of outcomes for a discussion can also pay off because it helps students stay on task. However, we must be flexible about adhering to these outlines. If important issues arise unexpectedly during discussions, we need to be prepared to abandon our preconceived notions of how the discussion will unfold. Moreover, because we want students to own more and more of the conversation, our goals ought to include transferring responsibility for the direction of conversations to students.

DISCUSSION CYCLES

Typically, discussions progress in a cycle that includes an introduction stage, a development stage, and a recapitulation and consolidation stage.

Introduction

During this stage, someone—a student or the teacher—presents a problem, issue or focus of inquiry. This usually involves more than simply saying something like, "Let's talk about health care in Great Britain." It may involve sharing background information or presenting questions designed to generate information or points of view that can provide a base for sharing ideas. For example, after listening to a speech about health care, the guiding question might be, What is the speaker's proposal and what strategies did she use to convince her audience that she has adopted the appropriate policy to solve the health-care crisis in the country?

Development

During this stage, answers to questions are posed and observations are made in response to the problem or questions presented. These answers are likely to need elaboration, exploration, examination and clarification, depending on the needs of the moment and the decisions of the participants in the discussion. For example, if someone says that a single-payer plan is the solution to the health-care crisis, someone else might ask for an explanation of this concept to ensure that everyone knows what is being discussed. Calls for clarification are often interspersed with moments of confrontation and challenge as students question one other, present evidence, and develop counter-arguments.

The questions asked as a discussion unfolds have an important impact on the effectiveness of discussions because they influence not only what students learn but also how much they learn. As a result, it's important to select questions carefully to spark specific responses. Here are some examples:

— *Reflect the answer back to the speaker*: "Did you just say that (rephrase what you think was said)?"
— *Expand an answer*: "Would you please expand or develop that answer a little more?"
— *Ask for clarification*: "I'm not sure I understand what you mean. Would you please clarify what you mean by...?"
— *Summarize what has been covered or discovered so far*: "We've explored several related ideas in the last few minutes. Could someone review what's been said up to this point?" This technique effectively draws in students who have been less active in the discussion.
— *Provide evidence or reasons for claims made*: "Can you provide evidence to back up that statement (or point of view)?"
— *Make a personal connection with the issue*: "Have you confronted or solved a similar problem in your own life? Have you known anyone who has?"
— *Elicit the opinion of others*: "Jennifer, what do you think about this solution (tactic, evidence, etc.)?"
— *Apply solutions*: "If we were to adopt and apply the solution we've been talking about, what would happen? What outcome would you expect? What problems might arise?"

While questions don't always fall into neat categories like these, they should broaden and deepen the inquiry rather than simply spark "correct" answers in the initiate-respond-evaluate tradition of teacher-talk. Effective questions focus attention and provide students with opportunities to make connections between the known and the unknown.

Recapitulation and Consolidation

This is the time for students and teacher to gather their thoughts, look back at what has been said, draw conclusions, state or restate discoveries, and form the foundation for another cycle of discussion.

TAKING TIME TO TALK ABOUT TALKING

Reflective learning can be fostered by focusing students' attention on their own thinking and how it might be improved. By examining their own thinking processes, students can discover how they think and, by internalizing effective thinking strategies, they learn how to think more proficiently. Encouraging students to talk about classroom dialogue is an excellent way of both heightening their awareness of thinking processes and encouraging them to acquire new tactics.

One way of doing this is to insert an additional stage—assessment—into the discussion cycle from time to time. This stage involves everyone in examining and evaluating the discourse to heighten their consciousness of what has worked and what might work better. The quality of this meta-discussion is often improved if students first write for a few minutes about the processes they've observed or meet in small groups to discuss them.

It often helps to pose a series of questions to guide this inquiry:

— What observations could you make about our discussion to help us see what happened more clearly?
— Did you observe any patterns in the interactions?
— How did we handle conflict over views or evidence?
— What responses or contributions helped the discussion progress unusually well?
— How might our discussion become more productive?

Although I recognize the importance of meta-discussions like these, I must often remind myself to pause and provide opportunities for them. The process helps students understand what's happening in the classroom, and helps me discover how they are experiencing the classroom dialogue, how deeply engaged they are, and how I might develop strategies to help deepen their involvement.

At times, these meta-discussions have sparked a restructuring or redirection of classroom activities—perhaps increasing the degree of student control over the content and purpose of the conversation. As students' capacity for social reasoning grows, they can assume more responsibility for and play more critical roles in choosing what and how to learn.

Robert Calfee, Kristy Dunlap and Albert Wat, who have studied classroom discourse, found that when students have more control over the content and direction of classroom conversations, they become more independent thinkers and learners. As a result, these researchers urge teachers to enable students to use their own resources and experiences to help shape the classroom curriculum. Giving students the opportunity—or obligation—to play a significant role in shaping the content of the curriculum appears to provide them with a chance to learn strategies for inquiry and methods of conducting authentic conversations.

Furthermore, the work of researchers like Matthew Keefer and Colleen Zeitz, who have studied conversational reasoning in children, indicates that their ability to reason improves if they are provided with a socially appropriate climate.

Follow-Up Activities

These small-group activities are intended to consolidate and extend students' learning about argumentative discourse by encouraging them to reflect on what they've learned and discover ways of transforming their knowledge.

— Describe a strategy—or use of language—that you learned about by studying everyday arguments.
— What are three important things you might tell someone about arguing (things you've discovered during our investigations or things you already knew that have been reconfirmed)? Why did you select these things?

— Compose 10 Commandments for more productive public discourse (e.g., Thou shalt not attack a person's character if you don't like that person's argument).

— Invent a new radio or TV show (include name, format and typical discussion issues) that includes the best features of all the shows you've seen or heard. Design it to appeal to teens (or children in your age group). Create and record a pilot.

— Design an inquiry project for the whole class that would lead to a deeper understanding of an everyday problem and help develop your critical thinking skills. Be ready to explain why the project should be undertaken and how it would contribute to the growth of critical thinking. (If time allows, one or more of these projects might be undertaken.)

— Demonstrate an aspect of argumentative discourse you've learned about, such as tactics teachers can use to encourage students to explore their ideas and feelings during discussions. Every group member must participate in the demonstration.

— Create manuals such as:
A Teenager's Guide to Arguing with Adults and Friends
An Adult's Guide to Arguing with Teenage Sons and Daughters
A Guide to Winning Arguments without Losing Friends
How to Handle Arguments with Girls (or Boys) (Is there a difference between the two?)

Conclusion

Developing an awareness of how we talk to one another, especially during arguments, can profoundly affect the quality and effectiveness of our communication. Much of this chapter focused on listening to and thinking about the ways people function during arguments. While proficient listening certainly enables teachers and students to engage in more thoughtful dialogue, effective questioning and discussion leadership can help us all deepen our inquiry and discovery. The following chapter shifts the focus to reading and explores strategies that teachers in all content areas can use to help students become more reflective and critical readers.

THINKING

THROUGH READING

Teachers play an important role in enriching the thinking that goes on as students are reading. To do this, however, it's important to understand what happens when people read. This understanding helps us develop strategies that contribute to the growth of more reflective readers and, therefore, thinkers and learners.

Reading: A Process of Constructing Meaning

Reading is a process of constructing meaning in which a reader interacts with a text, usually in a social context. The text provides "bottom-up" information to a reader in the form of symbols and signs that activate the reader's background knowledge and beliefs, which work in a "top-down" fashion. As the interaction between text and reader proceeds, the reader's cognitive and affective backgrounds influence the meanings that are constructed.

A reader's cognitive background includes world, literacy, metacognitive and personal knowledge. World knowledge comprises declarative (what-there-is) knowledge, procedural (how-to) knowledge and conditional (when-to-use-it) knowledge. Literacy knowledge includes knowledge of letters, sounds, words, grammar and text structure, all of which help us make sense of what we read. Metacognitive knowledge, which involves thinking about our thinking or knowledge construction processes, enables us to monitor and make decisions about strategies that help us read efficiently. Personal knowledge includes self-knowledge and memories drawn from our personal history.

A reader's affective background includes motivation, attitudes and values, and beliefs. Motivation refers to our desire or need to engage in reading. Attitudes and values refer to our preferences for people, places and things in the worlds we have constructed. And beliefs include the opinions and convictions that shape the decisions we make about the kind of life we want to live.

As we interact with texts during the reading process, our cognitive and affective backgrounds are selectively activated. If something interests us, our level of motivation may be high. For example, we may decide to read Eric Fromm's classic *The Art of Loving* because we're interested in developing our capacity for love. Our cognitive and affective backgrounds are activated as we think about the knowledge stimulated by the text, such as our knowledge of love and of ourselves as lovers. As we read, our literacy knowledge is activated and our metacognitive knowledge helps us pay attention to the meaning we're making to ensure that gaps are filled and misunderstandings are cleared up. These interdependent processes help us make sense of what we read.

Readers' Responses to Texts

Because every reader brings a unique background to a text, each produces his or her own unique meanings. In her transactional theory of reading, Louise Rosenblatt calls a reader's construction of a representation of a text its evocation. During and after constructing an evocation, Rosenblatt says that readers may adopt an efferent or an esthetic stance toward it.

Readers adopting an efferent—or scientific—stance, such as those reading instructions for filing an income-tax return, attend more to information, analysis and logic. Readers adopting an aesthetic—or artistic—stance, such as those reading a poem, enter the world of the text and focus more on its imaginative and emotional dimensions. An efferent stance tends to be public and shared; an aesthetic stance is more private and personal.

Adopting one of these stances, however, does not mean abandoning the other. Rosenblatt sees the efferent and the aesthetic stances as the two ends of a continuum, along which a reader may move while reading. For example, while reading *The Art of Loving,* someone may adopt a predominantly efferent stance at one stage, perhaps analyzing the components of genuine love as explained by Fromm. At a later stage, however, the same reader may adopt a more aesthetic stance, entering into and living through the emotional dimensions of Fromm's explanation of the kinds of love.

WHOSE MEANING IS CORRECT?

Those who accept Rosenblatt's perspective on reading expect that students will not only create different evocations of a text's meaning but may also adopt different stances toward those evocations at different times during the reading process. Clearly, this opens up the potential for the students in a single class to develop many different interpretations of the claims that arise from reading a text, whether this is a newspaper editorial or a surrealistic poem. If this is the case, how do we judge whether an interpretation is valid?

In fact, several interacting variables affect the validity of an interpretation of a text. In a classroom context, two of the most important are the source of authority and the kind of text.

Source of Authority

Reading experts have identified at least four competing sources of authority for interpreting texts in a classroom: the text, the individual reader, the teacher and the classroom community.

Those who assume that the meaning is in the text believe that the burden of discovering the meaning rests with the reader. The problem with this view is that it is often impossible to verify a meaning or prove that a single interpretation represents the author's purpose.

Others believe that the meaning of a text lies in the sense individual readers make of it. They hold that meaning is not inherent in a text; rather, it depends upon the background a reader brings to it. The problem with this view, which seems to suggest that every reader's response is equally valid, is that interpreting a text becomes a free for all.

In some classroom situations, the teacher's meaning is the only one that counts—and students are expected to accept the teacher's interpretation of what a text really means. The problem with this view is that it encourages students to rely on the teacher's claims about meaning, which may or may not be valid, rather than thinking about meaning for themselves.

In other classrooms, meaning is discovered through a consensus reached by discussing the text. In these interpretive communities, the text, individual readers and the teacher all contribute to classroom interactions that lead to the gelling of an accepted and acceptable interpretation. This view, too, has problems: the meanings constructed may be too relativistic— too dependent upon immediate contexts, such as culture and language.

Kind of Text

When considering the validity of an interpretation of a text, it's also important to take into account the kind of text. For example, imagine that a group of medical researchers who are investigating substitutes for human blood have just read an article describing a process discovered in another laboratory. The process purports to produce a blood substitute that not only does everything normal human blood does, but also bolsters the immune system of individuals fighting life-threatening diseases. The researchers are astonished and want to verify that the claims made in the article are accurate. How would they read the text? Certainly not as a poem, but as important information they require in order to replicate their colleagues' experiments. They assume that the meaning they seek is in the text and, if they can extract it, they can run the necessary experiments.

Or, imagine that the justices of the Supreme Court are faced with making an important decision about a civil rights law enacted in Wisconsin. Those opposed to the law say it contravenes the Constitution. On this basis, the Wisconsin Supreme Court has struck it down, but it was upheld by a federal Court of Appeals, which interpreted the Constitution differently. Now, the Supreme Court justices must decide which interpretation is correct. Clearly, they will not be applying exact scientific procedures to verify the claims of their colleagues.

Finally, imagine students in a literature class who have just read F. Scott Fitzgerald's *The Great Gatsby*. The teacher has asked them to write a paper interpreting the novel and explaining the reasons for their interpretation. The students are not conducting a scientific experiment in an attempt to replicate a procedure developed elsewhere, nor are they interpreting a legal document to determine if a law is constitutional. They're trying to make personal sense out of a work of imagination in a classroom context.

These examples drive home the significance of the kind of text in making decisions about whose interpretation really counts. Every text—scientific, legal or fictional—contains clues that indicate an author's purpose, whether this is to inform, persuade or tell a story. If readers recognize these clues, they can adopt a stance that is appropriate for the text.

According to Louise Rosenblatt, the stance adopted when reading a text influences how we decide on the validity of an interpretation. Efferent readings require public verification and confirmation. Aesthetic readings, which are more private and personal, rely on different standards that are often grounded in the affective domain.

Testing the Validity of Interpretations

With a teacher's guidance, students can engage in reasoned dialogue and debate to discover valid interpretations of text. To build classroom communities such as this, however, we need to shift from text- or teacher-centered instruction to reader-based instruction. We can do this by encouraging students to participate in authentic conversations about the meanings they have created in response to texts rather than relying on teacher-controlled question-and-answer routines.

Because there is a risk that the meanings constructed in these situations may be too relativistic, however, it's important to develop criteria for testing the validity of the interpretations that emerge. These criteria might include:

— The interpretation is the most complete or comprehensive in terms of the text's complexity.
— The interpretation permits the most extensive use of textual evidence.
— The interpretation is not contradicted by any statement in the text.
— The interpretation contains no contradictory statements.

— The interpretation best serves the purpose of the interpretive community (e.g., medical researchers who need an interpretation that enables them to perform appropriate verifying experiments).

While these criteria may be appropriate in many situations, they should always be open to revision as an interpretive community meets and talks about its purposes and the texts being read.

When students share responsibility for defining criteria and evolving valid interpretations during class discussions, they have an opportunity to reason reflectively about claims and persuade others of their validity. Of course, this process works only if the members of the interpretive community are cultivating a disposition to become critical thinkers.

Fostering a Transformative Outlook

Building interpretive classroom communities and establishing criteria for testing the validity of interpretations in these communities will not lead to absolute or irrefutable interpretations. Some students will still wonder if their interpretations, which may differ from those of others in the class, are valid. Some may even persuade a class to change its position on the meaning of a text. Interpretive communities are even likely to interpret the same text differently at different times.

How can teachers, as guides to negotiating meaning in interpretive communities, help students reach a valid consensus?

Those who hold a transformative outlook, which suggests that meanings evolve in cycles as evidence interacts with hypothesis, perception with theory, part with whole, and interpretation with assumption, believe that new meanings are always forming. Though it doesn't solve the problem of reconciling differing interpretations of a text, a transformative outlook helps us accept that no interpretation is permanent or static but is, rather, in a state of constant evolution. An interpretation cannot be stamped "objectively valid" because our cognitive and affective backgrounds, which we bring to each interpretive act, affect the meanings we construct. And these backgrounds are dynamic.

A transformative outlook enables us to explain to students that we are all engaged in a cycle of interpreting and re-interpreting meaning as we interact, assemble new knowledge, seek relevant standards, and search for good reasons for the meanings we construct. Our work is to discover the interpretations that are most valid according to our reason-based criteria.

Strategies for Promoting Reader-Based Responses

A variety of strategies can help build procedural knowledge that can contribute to the development of more reflective thinkers in interpretive classroom communities.

As Richard Beach suggested in *A Teacher's Introduction to Reader-Response Theories*, students may have many different perspectives on a text. By encouraging flexibility, teachers can enrich students' experiences with reading, support their development as reflective readers, and create classroom communities that foster the confident exploration of sense and reason. To build these communities, it's important to provide students with the time and opportunity to introduce their responses to the classroom conversation.

Reader-based responses fall into six main categories:

— Textual and intertextual responses.
— Cognitive responses.
— Metacognitive responses.
— Narrative responses.
— Affective responses.
— Socio-cultural responses.

TEXTUAL AND INTERTEXTUAL RESPONSES

Textual responses refer to readers' interactions with the conventions of a particular genre, such as poems, novels, autobiographies or arguments. Although the strategy described in the following material suggests that students work in groups to discover elements common to written arguments, it can be introduced as a whole-class activity if students seem to need more support. Once they have a better idea of what to look for, they can move on to the collaborative group activity.

Textual Features of Arguments

After organizing students into groups and selecting a discussion facilitator, recorder and reporter, give each group an argument to examine. I draw these from my argument archive, collected over the years, which contains letters to the editor, editorials from newspapers and magazines, and argumentative essays, both classical and current, on a wide range of issues. If the arguments are on different topics and from different sources, a variety of issues and approaches will be introduced when the groups report to the class.

Although students are likely to focus on the content of the argument at first, encourage them to identify features of the text that identify it as an argument. Guiding questions can help them do this:

— What purpose guides the author's writing?
— What features of the text lead to its classification as an argument?
— What pattern does the author use to arrange the text?
— What kind of introduction does the author use?
— What's happening in the first paragraph? In subsequent paragraphs?
— How does the author build or develop the text?
— Does the author introduce evidence and, if so, how?
— If the author states her or his position, when and how is this done?

As the group discovers the textual features, the recorder transcribes them. Once the groups have finished the assignment, the reporter presents the findings to the class and the teacher records them on the chalkboard. When all the groups have reported, the class can discuss the findings and students can record the features for their own information. A writing assignment in which students pull together the findings of the various groups and explain the features of the arguments examined makes an excellent follow-up.

Intertextual Connections

A second strategy focuses on intertextual links, the connections readers make between the text that is being read and texts stored in their memories. These links are not limited to printed texts, such as novels, poems or editorials; rather, they can include links to movies, plays, news events, songs and so on. Often unaware of these enriching connections, readers, especially younger ones, tend to approach the reading of a new argument without considering other texts that relate to it, even though these intertextual links may significantly shape the meanings they are constructing.

To encourage students to explore these links, ask them to draw a cluster, web or map that shows the connections between the topic of the argument and other "texts" they may have experienced. Encourage them to keep this paper handy so that they can add links that come to mind as they read. For example, if students are reading an argument in favor of a policy to reduce crime, they might draw upon their crime-text repertoire, including movies, books and news stories about crime and crime prevention.

Once students have finished reading the selection and drawing their intertextual maps, suggest that they gather in small groups to discuss the associated texts, then write a piece focusing on the intertextual links.

To ensure that students have plenty of scope for making these intertextual links, it's a good idea to start with topics they can readily relate to, such as critiques of movies or popular musicians, censorship arguments and other issues relevant to their age group. It's worth noting, however, that students' intertextual links may be more plentiful than we think. When students in one of my classes were reading Ralph Waldo Emerson's "Self Reliance," for example, I asked them to be alert to connections they could make between Emerson's argument in favor of individualism and other texts. With little prompting, they generated many intertextual connections to Emerson's central idea.

An alternative strategy involves giving students a packet of arguments on the same issue, such as gun control, and asking them to read all the arguments and construct a map of the intertextual links among them. Several publishers now issue books, such as the Taking Sides series, and pamphlets presenting alternative views of controversial issues (see "Resources"). A simple notational system can help designate which information came from which argument.

Cognitive responses are made by readers when they construct meaning or build a text representation. While cognitive responses are essential to any meaning-making process, they are especially important when dealing with argumentative texts. Although many cognitive processes occur during reading, this section focuses on world knowledge stored in schemata, the hypothesized mental structures that contain networks of related knowledge that help us shape the meanings we construct. Although world knowledge may be declarative, procedural or conditional, the strategies presented here are designed to activate students' declarative knowledge before they read a text. Additional strategies can be designed to activate other forms of knowledge.

Activating Background Knowledge

Because reflective thinkers are active as well as reactive, it helps to encourage students to activate their background knowledge, about both an author and a topic, before they read a text. Although students knowledge of particular authors is often limited, their knowledge of topics is usually broader and may be effectively tapped by using a variety of writing-to-read strategies. For example, I've often asked students to write everything they know about the topic of an essay before they actually read it. This 10-minute exercise generates information that can be shared in small groups and with the class before the argument is read.

Or, I might suggest that they work in pairs to tell each other everything they know about a topic. Depending on the students' ability and the time available, each pair then discusses a feature of arguments, such as the thesis, and creates one for the topic. The partners might also plan how they would defend their position in an essay, develop arguments to persuade others to their position, delineate evidence that might be used to support a thesis, and anticipate the form a counter-argument might take. This approach not only activates previous knowledge, but also generates predictions about the content of the argument they are about to read.

One of the most effective strategies for encouraging students to make predictions is the directed reading-thinking activity, developed by Russell Stauffer. Before introducing an essay or argument, I distribute a sheet of blank paper that is used to cover the text as I guide a silent reading. I ask students to begin by covering all the text except the title. Then, based on the title, I ask them to predict what the reading will be about. I encourage as many predictions as possible, asking questions to encourage students to clarify their suggestions. For example, students who were about to read Henry David Thoreau's "On the Duty of Civil Disobedience" came up with a variety of predictions. Some predicted that the essay would be a satire on demonstrators, probably environmentalists, while others came very close to Thoreau's thesis, suggesting that it would be about the importance of following your own beliefs even if governments don't agree with you. The students' predictions can be confirmed or discarded as the reading progresses.

Once we've discussed the title, I ask students to read the first paragraph. Then I ask if their predictions have been confirmed, and encourage them to make additional predictions. We continue the reading in this way, pausing at appropriate points to confirm or discard predictions and make new ones. Along the way, I sometimes introduce other questions designed to focus students' thinking on evidence, assumptions, analogies and other important features of an argument.

To give students an opportunity to practice predicting and planning for writing, I sometimes stop in the middle of a DRTA and ask them to imagine that they are the writer and explain what they would write next if it were up to them.

DRTAs enable students to make predictions about a text without worrying about whether they're right or wrong. Their background knowledge is activated and their motivation to read is heightened because they want to know whether their predictions are accurate. When they finish reading, I often ask them to reflect on their responses in writing and to draw a map, diagram or picture to represent their response. These maps are shared and discussed with a partner or the whole class.

Another effective strategy is K-W-L, developed by Donna Ogle. This involves folding a blank page to make three columns. The first is labeled What I Know (K); the second is labeled What I Want to Know (W); and the third is labeled What I Learned (L). Before starting the reading, students record what they know about the topic in the first column and what they'd like to know about the topic—and claims related to it—in the second column. I encourage them to include questions about the structure of the argument, assumptions, evidence and reasoning (e.g., Does the author present convincing evidence for his positions as well as counter-arguments to challenge them?). After reading the article, students record in the third column what they learned about the topic, as well as notes about the design and features of the argument. We then discuss what they knew, what they wanted to know, and what they learned about the substance of the argument and the author's method.

Summarizing Arguments

Students who can effectively summarize and assess the significance of an argument have acquired two valuable cognitive and academic skills. Mapping is an effective technique for helping students learn how to identify and record the main points of an argument. To make a map of an argument, they usually begin by writing the topic in the center of the map and arranging claims, counter-claims, evidence and implied assumptions in a network around this hub. These clusters can become quite elaborate as students include assumptions the writer has made, their questions about evidence given, additional information that can be added to the argument, or problems in the structure of the argument.

A dialogue profile is a technique that works well with younger students or those just beginning to read argumentative prose. The teacher gives students a picture of two human profiles facing each other. After reading an argument, the students write in one profile the author's position as they understand it, including major claims and evidence. In the other, they write a counter-argument, either as it is developed in the article or as they would develop it themselves or both. These dialogue profiles can then be shared with partners, discussed in class, and displayed.

METACOGNITIVE RESPONSES

When we monitor our reading, pay attention to breakdowns in the reading process, activate strategies to fix these breakdowns, or assess our likelihood of success before starting a complex reading or learning assignment, we are engaging in metacognitive activities. We're thinking about our own thinking. Thinking about our cognitive potential and processes helps us make effective choices about how to use our knowledge-constructing powers, understand tasks and keep track of the sense we are making of our experience. Teachers who actively try to help students develop their metacognitive knowledge promote reflective thinking.

Metacognition Questionnaire

To explore how extensively students activate their own metacognitive processes when reading, I've designed a questionnaire on metacognition. This helps me both understand what students know about their thinking while they are reading and design exercises to build their metacognitive awareness.

Because metacognition involves self-knowledge, self-management and self-assessment, the survey questions fall into these categories. I try to discuss students' answers to the questions so that those with greater metacognitive awareness and a wider repertoire of strategies can serve as models for others.

1. What are your strengths and weaknesses as a reader? How did you gain the strengths you have as a reader? How could you improve in your weak areas?
2. What kinds of reading do you enjoy most?
3. What kinds of reading do you enjoy least?
4. What do you do, if anything, to prepare yourself mentally before beginning to read? Do you ever skim? When? How? Do you ever read headings in advance? When?
5. About what percentage of the time that you are reading do you sense that you are monitoring or observing your understanding of your reading?
6. What are three things that influence the quality of your reading?
7. What do you do to manage your thinking while reading an English, history or science book?
8. When you are reading and come across a word you don't understand, what do you usually do?
9. What do you usually do when you come across a whole sentence or paragraph you don't understand?

10. When you find yourself completely unable to follow and understand what you're reading, what do you do?
11. Under what conditions or circumstances would you give up on a reading assignment?
12. Do you read at a variety of rates or just one? If you read at a variety of rates, for what kinds of reading do you use your fastest rate? Your slowest rate? What rate do you enjoy most?
13. Do you usually pause to summarize what you've read or ask yourself questions? When reading, how do you know when it's time to summarize? What kinds of questions do you usually ask yourself?
14. When reading an argument that challenges your opinions, values or beliefs, do you reflect on challenging evidence the author has stated or presented? If so, what do you look for? If not, how do you deal with your sense of disagreement?

Reciprocal Reading

Reciprocal reading, a one-on-one strategy developed by Ann Brown, Annemarie Palincsar and Bonnie Armbruster, involves the teacher in modeling metacognitive processes, such as summarizing, predicting, clarifying and questioning. The strategy helps students focus on their own thinking by monitoring, managing and assessing their progress in constructing meaning as they read arguments. The assumption is that they will internalize these processes so that they can use them on their own.

Once both the teacher and a student have silently read a passage, the teacher summarizes what was read and asks the student to answer a question about the content, make a prediction, or clarify the meaning of a word, phrase, sentence or concept. The teacher and student then read another passage and exchange roles. This time, the student summarizes the passage and asks the teacher a question. Although students may struggle at first to summarize or ask "teacher-like" questions, they soon catch on. This strategy can be adapted for use with small groups or even a whole class by asking individual students to take turns exchanging roles with the teacher or even another student.

When using this technique to encourage critical thinking, I begin by summarizing and asking basic questions. Soon, however, I introduce more challenging questions designed to promote deeper analysis. For example, I might ask questions that focus on the assumptions writers make, on the evaluation of claims, or on the inferences that can be drawn from a passage. When we exchange roles, I encourage the students to ask me more challenging questions, too.

NARRATIVE RESPONSES

Narrative responses refer to the personal stories and images sparked by reading a specific text. These may include memories such as a family birthday party, an encounter with a loving aunt, or a fight with a friend.

To draw out these responses, students are encouraged to report an autobiographical event associated with a reading. For example, after reading an argument about controlling pollution in our oceans, one student who was an avid surfer wrote about his experiences with sewage in the surf. His vivid imagery left no doubt about the importance of this topic to him.

Although I tend to use this strategy when dealing with topics that I'm sure will spark responses from all the students, I keep a backup assignment ready for those who can't think of anything related to the argument we've read. This often involves suggesting that they write about someone else's experience.

AFFECTIVE RESPONSES

One way of activating students' affective responses before reading an argument is to ask them to develop a brief position paper on the topic. In the paper, students state their opinion and their reasons for holding it. For example, they might describe and defend their positions on capital punishment or sex education. Doing this clarifies their beliefs before they do the reading and engage in discussion. After sharing their position papers in class, students read the argument. We then review features of the argument that either confirmed or led them to re-examine their personally held assumptions and beliefs.

When I taught in a northern California high school, some students were trying to persuade the school board to adopt an "open-campus" policy at lunch so they could go into town. Because other students favored a closed campus, feelings ran high on both sides of the issue. Before inviting the students in one of my classes to read a newspaper editorial opposing the policy, I asked them to write a brief paper stating—and backing up—their positions on the issue. Before reading the editorial, we talked about what they had written, an exercise that helped them discuss the issue more clearly after the reading. I often conclude by asking students to answer this question in their learning logs: Which of your beliefs or values were confirmed or challenged by the argument?

SOCIO-CULTURAL RESPONSES

Socio-cultural responses reflect a reader's roles in the family, school, community or wider culture. To encourage students to discover more about themselves as social and cultural agents, teachers can encourage them to focus on how they respond in the classroom. Questions such as the following can serve as a springboard to further exploration of the way social roles and cultural traditions shape readers' responses in the classroom.

— In what kinds of school situations (talking to friends, working in a science lab, listening to a math lecture, talking about a book, attending a club meeting, participating in sports, sharing in school government, etc.) do you think you are at your best? Why?
— In what ways has your family influenced the way you function as a student or reader? How do you think your family's attitudes toward school and schooling influence your own?
— Are there cliques in this school? If so, how do you think they influence the behavior of the students who belong to them? Do you see yourself as a member of a clique? Do you think membership in a group influences the way group members respond to school? To reading or discussing ideas in school? Please explain your answers.
— Do you behave differently in different classrooms? If so, why?

— What does it mean to you to be a student in this particular classroom?
— How does the structure of this class define the way you respond to the texts we read or our discussions?
— When you are a member of a group talking about your reactions to something we've read, how do you usually behave? What do you typically do?
— To what degree do you see yourself as responsible for helping to form and share a meaning for something we've read in class? For persuading others of the validity of your interpretations? For finding evidence in the text to support your interpretations?
— How do you prefer to respond to texts in this class and why?
— Do you think being male or female influences the way you respond to arguments that you read and discuss in small groups or with the whole class?

A Typical Reading Lesson

Because the argument selected for a lesson is so important, it's a good idea to choose it carefully. I've had good luck with topics in which students feel they have something at stake, such as editorials about censorship or youth service projects. However, the argument selected depends very much on the needs, interests and abilities of a particular group of students.

I usually begin with a writing activity designed to encourage students to activate their previous knowledge of a topic. This helps them understand that what they bring to an argument influences what they take from it. Then I ask them to indicate their position on the topic—for, against, unknown, uncommitted or abstaining—through a show of hands and record the results of this survey on the chalkboard.

The students then read the argument and respond in writing using one of the strategies suggested earlier.

We then move into the discussion phase of the lesson, which involves clarifying the writer's thesis. As students offer their interpretations of the claim, I write these on the chalkboard. The students then identify evidence supporting the thesis. To encourage as much participation as possible, I often ask them to contribute in turn until we've exhausted the possibilities.

To include those who didn't have a chance to participate in this, I might ask the others to summarize or restate each point as I record it on the chalkboard.

If necessary, I model the rephrasing process and offer guidance as students learn listening and recapping skills. Rephrasing the evidence helps them reflect on it independently and ensures that they understand it. At this stage, I encourage everyone to watch for the influence of background knowledge on the evidence students say they found in the text. This helps ensure that the evidence cited is actually in the text.

Once we've completed this phase, I suggest that students come up with other reasons for supporting the thesis. These are recorded on the chalkboard in brackets to show that they weren't drawn from the text.

Next, the students select the evidence they consider the most persuasive and explain their choice in writing. I poll them to discover which they favored, and we discuss the criteria for their selections. This enables us to explore the judgments they've made and examine assumptions about the kind of evidence or reasoning that is most effective, an activity that helps them develop their metacognitive knowledge.

I then ask students to identify an antithesis, alternative position, or counter-argument in the reading selection and cite evidence that could be used to support it. This involves repeating the process of finding and summarizing the evidence, then adding evidence that is not included in the text.

If no antithesis or counter-argument is included in the selection, I invite students to suggest one or more and back them up with reasons. Just as we did with the thesis, we decide which evidence supporting the antithesis is the most persuasive.

Once we have thoroughly examined both the thesis and the antithesis, the students evaluate the two and decide which is most persuasive. Another poll of the class shows whether any opinions have changed as a result of the reading and discussion. As we discuss their reasons for sticking with or changing their original views on the topic, the students have an opportunity to reflect on the reasons for their decisions and learn more about their own thinking.

The process of argument analysis described in this section can serve as an introduction to a more independent form of argument analysis called TASK, which will be introduced in the next chapter.

Conclusion

When reading, we conduct meanings on which to reflect and, through reasoned reflection, we critically inspect interpretations to discover their worth. In classroom communities that encourage reader-based strategies, students make, share and evaluate their interpretations. Interpretive communities enable us to promote the examination of claims and thoughtful actions based upon them.

The next chapter explores a procedure called TASK, which is designed to improve students' ability to interpret and assess arguments.

THINKING THROUGH READING

WITH TASK

To help students learn to reflect independently on the features of an argumentative essay, I have developed a strategy called TASK, an acronym for thesis-analysis-synthesis key. While this chapter focuses on TASK as a guide to reading critically, its uses as a guide for writing are explored in the following chapters.

Used as part of the process of reading argumentative prose, TASK encourages students to adopt an efferent stance that helps them construct meaningful, coherent text representations. As they identify and examine the claims and evidence that make up arguments, seek valid reasons to support claims and counter-claims, envision arguments from different points of view, and engage in a dialectical process while reading arguments, TASK fosters the development and internalization of critical thinking skills.

And because TASK involves students in responding to texts as both readers and collaborators with the writers, it helps them make connections between reading and writing arguments. The collaboration is generated when readers suggest ideas that supplement, evaluate or challenge the writer's argument. In addition, TASK encourages readers to connect sympathetically but critically with the writer's values and beliefs.

I found that using TASK significantly improved students' ability to read and assess an argument. This improvement was most evident in their ability to recognize weaknesses in arguments, such as irrelevant material, lack of supporting reasons, fallacies of partiality, and improper appeals to authority. Their ability to write arguments also improved.

The procedure was more effective when students worked in mixed-ability, cooperative groups than when we worked as a whole class. In the groups, which usually included one high-achiever, one low-achiever, and two average achievers, group members helped each other learn and apply the procedure by talking through the phases of the strategy and explaining them to one other.

What Is TASK?

Essentially, TASK is a series of 10 questions that help guide students' reading and writing of an argument.

1. What topic is being judged?
2. What basic claim is made about this topic?
3. Identify a counter-claim: What would a reader who opposes the claim most likely be for or against?
4. What supports the basic claim and the counter-claim? List these supports in separate columns.
5. Does the piece include any unclear, complex or "loaded" language? If so, identify and clarify it.
6. Evaluate the supports for both the claim and the counter-claim. Identify questionable inferences, irrelevant supports, fallacies and other weaknesses in the argument.
7. Do you recognize any assumptions, values or ideological influences in the basic claim or its supports? Identify these and state whether they affect the validity of the claim.
8. State the full claim in the following form: Although ...(fill in the counter-claim or one of its strongest supports), ... (fill in the basic claim) because ... (fill in a major cause for belief in the basic claim).
9. Is the full thesis debatable yet supportable beyond a reasonable doubt, insupportable, or too complex to support?
10. If necessary, revise your statement of the basic claim and repeat the phases of TASK.

These questions are printed on a single sheet of paper that contains room for students to record their answers.

To help students learn to use TASK, I developed a booklet tailored to the backgrounds, interests and abilities of the particular students. Teachers, too, can learn a great deal while preparing the booklet and trying it out. If time doesn't allow this, a variety of introductory texts on critical thinking contain activities that can be adapted for classroom use (see "Resources").

The first part of the booklet clarified the nature of arguments and outlined several types of claims. The second introduced extended arguments, including inductive, deductive and analogical patterns of argument, while the third focused on the finer features of arguments, especially fallacies of relevance, ways of analyzing arguments, and qualities of effective arguments. The final sections introduced TASK and demonstrated how to use it.

THE PHASES OF TASK

Each of the questions listed earlier represents one phase of TASK. Keeping these in mind makes reading arguments more purposeful, active and fruitful.

Because readers interpret texts differently, students' responses to the questions vary. However, continuing interaction with the text, dialogues between teacher and students, and class discussions help clarify an author's meaning, a reader's evocation, and a classroom community's understanding. Using TASK as a guide to reading is a recursive process, one that is open to change as meanings are created and recreated.

To show students how TASK works, I choose arguments that focus on topics related to their world. I also invite them to keep an eye out for effective—or even ineffective—arguments and bring these to class.

When teaching students to use TASK, I introduce each phase with sample exercises such as the following:

What topic is being judged in this passage?

Stormy debates rage over the kind and amount of the media's effects on the individual and on society. It would be easy to let the problem of media education collapse beneath the weight of these controversies. Unable to decide whether to teach that TV is a mechanical device that destroys brain cells and deadens our spirits or that TV is our portal to a communications network embodying human potential to expand minds and lift spirits, we don't teach anything at all. The obvious solution, suggested by educators in other contexts, is to teach the controversies: describe the poles of opinion, investigate, analyze, locate the reasons to care, and, in doing so, vivify a public issue that badly needs a little life.

Don Adams & Arlene Goldbarb
The Independent Film & Video Monthly: Aug.-Sept., 1989.

Phase 1—What topic is being judged?

Although identifying the topic might seem straightforward, it isn't always as easy as it first appears. Titles don't always offer clues and writers sometimes don't set out this information clearly until later in a piece. Nevertheless, taking the time to find an essay's central topic can prevent confusion as readers begin to unravel the argument.

At this stage, it's important to emphasize that students are not expected to describe or judge the topic. Nothing more or less than the topic should be stated.

Phase 2—What basic claim is made about this topic?

I encourage students to record the basic claim or thesis as precisely as possibly in their own words. The thesis can be any of several types of claim—fact, moral, policy, interpretive, etc.

In some texts, finding the basic claim or thesis is easy. In others, however, it may be hidden or implied so that the reader must dig it out.

Phase 3—Identify a counter-claim: What would a reader who opposes the claim likely be for or against?

The counter-claim, or antithesis, is a claim that challenges or contradicts the basic claim. If the text doesn't include an antithesis, students formulate one and record it in brackets to remind them that it's their own.

Doing this encourages students to examine an argument from an opposing point of view and helps develop their awareness of the tension that creates debate and discussion. Moreover, looking at an issue from various perspectives helps them form their own theses, antitheses and extended arguments.

To help students hone this skill, I often present a series of statements similar to the following and ask them to express the antithesis:

— Students today are too ambitious.
— Initiatives such as affirmative action programs should be introduced to bring the incomes of visible minorities into line with those of the white majority.
— You can lead a horse to water, but you can't make him drink. (Suggestion: Express this adage in your own words, then state the antithesis in your own words.)
— A bird in the hand is worth two in the bush.
— Free speech should have no limits.
— The rise in racist and sexist remarks threatens free speech on campuses throughout our country.
— Increasing government regulations are strangling freedom.
— The feminist movement has created more freedom of choice for women—especially young women—than they ever would have achieved without it.
— Goodness of action arises only from nobility of goals.

Phase 4—What supports the basic claim and the counterclaim? List these supports in separate columns.

Supports are evidence or reasons that back up claims. They include examples, generalizations induced from the evidence, the findings of experiments and surveys, inferences, deductive conclusions, stories, symptoms, facts, comparisons (including metaphors and analogies), statements from authorities, and more.

At this stage, I encourage students to list all the supports they can, without worrying about quality. I also encourage them to come up with supports the author may have overlooked, listing these in brackets to signal that they were not included in the text. Because space on the TASK sheet is limited, students can do this on the back of the page.

The following is an example of a reading selection that can help them master this skill:

Television makes positive contributions to many populations. Children discover how to improve in school and in their social worlds. Older people get information about problems related to health, retirement and community concerns while being kept company. Minority groups use it to gain access to the majority culture and to become attuned to new cultures while keeping in touch with their own heritage. People in institutions, such as hospitals or prisons, reduce their sense of isolation from the larger society and acquire both skills and information.

Adapted from *Big World, Small Screen*
by Aletha Huston et al.

Phase 5—Does the piece include any unclear, complex, or "loaded" language? If so, identify and clarify it.

If students have come across any unfamiliar, unclear or ambiguous words, they define and clarify them during this phase. If, for example, a writer claims that psychotherapy is effective, readers need to define the meaning of both "psychotherapy" and "effective." To analyze and evaluate an argument such as this, readers need to know precisely what these terms mean.

They also identify words and concepts that reveal a writer's bias. To help them do this, we talk about loaded language, which often signals hidden assumptions and reveals prejudices. For example, we might discuss how using words like "pill-pusher" for doctor or "ambulance-chaser" for lawyer can obscure the fair-minded consideration of a topic.

Examples like the following help students master this phase. I usually ask them to try to restate each sentence so that its meaning is clearer and more free of bias.

— Psychological death squads bent on getting their way on environmental issues have terrorized American oil companies.
— The nuclear power industry has desecrated the land with reactors.
— Baby rabbits have been sacrificed at the altar of the cosmetics industry to test a new skin lotion.
— By preventing important research, animal rights activists threaten to cripple drug companies that are laboring to test beneficial medicines.

Phase 6—Evaluate the supports for both the claim and the counter-claim. Identify questionable inferences, irrelevant supports, fallacies and other weaknesses in the argument.

With the groundwork laid, students are ready to analyze the argument critically. This analysis involves evaluating the supports for both the claim and the counter-claim, as well as the relationship between them and the supports. The students identify errors in inductive, deductive or analogical reasoning, and look for over-generalizations, questionable inferences, faulty premises and false analogies, as well as fallacies of relevance, such as jumping on a bandwagon, name-calling, throwing in red herrings, making improper appeals to authority, and appealing to prejudice or tradition. We also identify fallacies of partiality, which occur when a writer withholds important elements of an argument or tries to shift the burden of proof to the reader. Again, because their notes may be extensive, I suggest that students record them on the back of the page.

Strongly worded pieces like the following, which advocates doing away with compulsory schooling, provide rich opportunities for the kind of analysis required by this phase. When a piece is long, as this one is, I number the paragraphs to help students keep track and suggest that they write letters in response.

In their responses, I instruct them to identify the thesis, explain the strengths and weaknesses of each paragraph, and, in a final paragraph, state whether the entire argument is weak or strong and why. I remind them that their opinion of the substance of the arguments is not the important thing at this stage; rather, their focus should be on analyzing and evaluating the quality of the reasoning.

Compulsory schooling, which now forces children to attend school to the age of 16, should be eliminated. Students should attend school only if they want to.

To force children to attend school is to send them to prison. It is illegal to send anyone to prison without a trial. Therefore, requiring children to attend school should be against the law.

The minister of education has argued in his own foolish way that compulsory schooling is essential if we are to have a free society. What fool's logic! Compulsory freedom is a contradiction. Don't let this fool fool you.

Compulsory schooling wastes resources. If children were not forced to attend school, time and money could be saved. Fewer staff members would be needed because they would not have to spend time on attendance procedures, such as dealing with truancy. The money saved could be used for instruction.

Children love to play after school and on weekends, when playgrounds and playing fields are crowded. The younger ones play on swings, slides and climbing structures. The older ones play baseball, football, tennis and other sports. They all have a good time.

If compulsory schooling is prohibited, children will be happier. All intelligent citizens regard the happiness of children as highly desirable. So, we should all be in favor of ending compulsory schooling.

Last year, the superintendent of schools conducted an experiment that proves that compulsory schooling should be eliminated. For a full month, he allowed two 14-year-old students, a boy and a girl, to decide for themselves whether they wanted to go to school. At the end of the month, the two reported that they had learned more and were happier than when they were forced to go to school.

A prominent professor of education has recommended that compulsory schooling be ended. And a major child-development organization has made the same recommendation.

Finally, opponents of this proposal have said that compulsory schooling is necessary to prepare children for life in our complex society. These people do not know what "schooling" really means. It means letting kids be where they want, have jobs and enjoy themselves. Compulsory schooling does nothing to school children.

Phase 7—Do you recognize any assumptions, values or ideological influences in the basic claim or its supports? Identify these and state whether they affect the validity of the claim.

To ensure that they are able to do this, we define assumptions, values and ideologies, and identify features that indicate their presence in arguments. Knowing that writers' perceptions can be colored by their beliefs enables readers to evaluate the quality of an argument.

As students identify the biases identified in the previous phase, they can record their responses on the back of the TASK sheet.

Here is an example of an analysis of the assumptions and values underlying Ralph Waldo Emerson's statement "Imitation is suicide" from his essay "Self-Reliance."

Emerson assumes, for one, that his readers will understand that by "imitation" he means conformity and that by "suicide" he means spiritual or mental suffocation. He implies that to develop oneself as a unique individual is a more important goal than to emulate others. The ideology reflected in the quotation is that of individualism.

Note that this analysis does not assess the validity of Emerson's statement. This is not the purpose of this phase: it is to help students learn more about how values and beliefs can shape arguments.

The depth of students' analysis often varies. For those who are just beginning to analyze arguments, merely identifying stated values may be a challenge. Those with better-developed skills, however, may be able to delve deeper to find implied values.

This phase—and the previous one—are often the most difficult for students. As they dig beneath a writer's surface language to scrutinize values, represented by words like "good," they begin to discover that understanding all the nuances of language takes care and time. The effort is worthwhile, however, because knowledge of an author's assumptions, values and ideological beliefs enlarges our understanding of an argument.

Quotations like the following can help introduce students to this phase of TASK:

— Reason is the greatest enemy that faith has....
Martin Luther, leader of the Reformation in Germany
— Through clever and constant application of propaganda, people can be made to see paradise as hell, and also the other way round, to consider the most wretched sort of life as paradise.
Adolph Hitler, Nazi leader
— New opinions are always suspected, and usually opposed, without any other reason but because they are not already common.
John Locke, English philosopher

— The only freedom which deserves the name, is that of pursuing our own good in our own way, so long as we do not attempt to deprive others of theirs, or impede their efforts to obtain it.
John Stuart Mill, English philosopher

— We are advocates of the abolition of war; we do not want war, but war can only be abolished through war, and in order to get rid of the gun it is necessary to take up the gun.... When classes and states are eliminated, there will be no more wars.
Mao Tse-tung, leader of the Chinese Communist State

— Intuitively or not, (leaders) seem to sense that the heart and soul are far greater energizers than the mind and logic.
Jay A. Conger, author of The Charismatic Leader

The following is another activity that encourages students to recognize and analyze assumptions, values and beliefs:

The left and right—or liberal and conservative—ends of the political spectrum are often seen as different ideologies; that is, as systems of values that express a specific vision. These ideological camps often take opposing views on issues. Generate a list of controversial issues, such as health care, abortion, capital punishment, gun control, the welfare system, taxation and so on, and state claims about those topics that are typical of the liberal and conservative camps. What are the risks to reason of belonging to a camp?

Phase 8—State the full claim in the following form: Although ...(fill in the counter-claim or one of its strongest supports), ...(fill in the basic claim) because...(fill in a major cause for belief in the basic claim).

As students combine three related elements identified in previous phases into this pattern, they not only learn to distill an argument, but also practice combining ideas, a skill they will need when they begin formulating their own thesis statements.

Here is an example of the procedure. After reading an essay on grades, a student might have written the following on her TASK sheet:

Basic claim: Grades should be abolished.
Basic claim support: Grades are worthless indicators of real learning.
Counter-claim or counter-claim support: Grades provide schools and colleges with a means of measuring a student's achievement.

She would then combine these elements into this statement:

Although grades provide schools and colleges with a means of measuring students' achievement, they should be abolished because they are worthless indicators of real learning.

It's worth noting that condensing a complex argument into a statement like this can distort an author's position. As a result, teachers need to help students capture the essentials when condensing arguments. At the same time, because students' interpretations of the essentials may differ, we need to encourage thoughtful discussion of these. Despite the risks, combining the fundamental elements of an argument into this format seems to help students grasp and evaluate the overall quality of a writer's argument.

To help students practice this skill, I might present them with a series of statements such as the following and invite them to formulate the patterned statement:

Basic claim: More restrictive gun control laws won't reduce violent crimes.
Basic claim support: People assassinate—not guns.
Counter-claim or counter-claim support: Hand guns have been used in the assassinations or attempted assassination of many public officials.

Basic claim: A flat tax should be enacted.
Basic claim support: Taxpayers wouldn't be able to take advantage of tax loopholes.
Counter-claim or counter-claim support: The poor should be taxed at a lower rate than the wealthy.

Basic claim: *The Sun Also Rises* is Hemingway's finest novel.
Basic claim support: *The Sun Also Rises* captures in resonant prose the loneliness, desperation and waste of a generation of Americans.

Counter-claim or counter-claim support: A Farewell to Arms depicts a tragic loss of love and life.

And here is a follow-up activity:

Reformulate two of the statements created in the previous exercise so that the counter-claim becomes the claim. Develop a reasonable argument to support the new thesis, and state it in the same pattern.

Phase 9—Is the full thesis debatable yet supportable beyond a reasonable doubt, insupportable, or too complex to support?

This phase, which guides students toward drawing fundamental conclusions about a writer's thesis, helps them understand that a basic claim should merit a reader's thoughtful consideration.

Phase 10—If necessary, revise your statement of the original claim and repeat the phases of TASK.

This phase, which provides students with an opportunity to revise a basic claim and reconstruct an argument if they think the original claim could be stated and supported more effectively, accentuates the transformative aspect of critical thinking. Furthermore, revising someone else's arguments helps students recognize that some of their own arguments may require extensive revision.

To illustrate this point, I once presented the following argument in favor of abolishing grades to two classes of students, many of whom were having trouble evaluating the validity of arguments. In addition to this essay, which I had written myself, I also asked them to read an article from the *New York Times*. This carefully researched and documented article presented an opposing point of view.

The assignment was simple: read the two articles and decide which argument is more effective.

In all the talk of fixing the publicly funded school system, we rarely hear about the one thing that would vastly improve education in this country: eliminating grades.

Grades are like the Wizard of Oz—imposing and oppressive, but total illusion. They give us no information that is truly important. They tell us nothing about what is really inside students' minds. Some students who get

A's may get a brief ego-boost, while others may feel that these grades are empty and meaningless. Some who get Ds or Fs may feel like failures, while others may feel that their Fs don't accurately measure their achievement and are unworthy of a moment's thought. Some students with straight A's may feel stupid all the time, while some with Cs or Ds may feel like the smartest kid in sight.

For the most part, students view grades the way little children view candy: they beg—and even cry—for them. In the end, however, just as candy rots teeth, grades rot genuine motivation and learning. This is because students become addicted to grades and look upon them as addicts might look upon a drug they desperately need to feel good again.

Most of the brightest students in our best universities long ago saw the Wizard of Oz for what he really is, and now see that grades, too, are simply attempts by the established powers to maintain control over their weaker subjects—the students. The best of our university professors see through the grade fantasy also. So when are the kids in our high schools, like university students, going to wise up to the tokenism of grades?

If high school students are serious about gaining independence, becoming adults and maturing, it's time they shook off the chains of the grading system. The current system encourages students to become slaves building monuments of letters. Every day, with their chains clattering, they drag themselves from class to class in pursuit of points, extra credit, or a sign of approval from their taskmasters. Some are crushed by the work. Some come to hate the other slaves who struggle to achieve success or become lost slave-zombies, dead on the inside. Others become cynics and their cynicism lulls them into believing that they have gained the upper hand over their peers and their masters.

So, what is to be done if we are serious about our own learning? End the tyranny of the grade! Bring the reign of the letter to an end!

After reading both arguments, without subjecting them to the kind of analysis required by TASK, the students in both classes overwhelmingly voted my argument superior to that presented by the *Times*. This opinion, which, I suspect, says much about the appeal of emotion, was shared by 27 of 28 students in one class and 24 of 27 in the other.

I then asked the students to analyze each argument using TASK. By the time they had finished, most of them had changed their minds about which was most effective.

Conclusion

Using TASK to analyze arguments provides students with a logical structure that helps them identify claims, organize and evaluate supports, and recognize assumptions, values and beliefs. It's worth noting, however, that it isn't appropriate to use this strategy to analyze every argument. Some arguments are too long; some too complex; and some too technical. Nevertheless, learning to apply TASK provides students with an important resource to guide reflection on aspects of nearly any argument. Perhaps even more important, though, using TASK to analyze arguments written by others helps prepare students to use the process to formulate and support their own theses, a process that will be explored in the next two chapters.

. . . .

THINKING

THROUGH WRITING

Researchers have found that writing analytical essays involves more higher-order thinking than many other learning tasks, such as note-taking or answering questions. When writing analytical essays, students generate more complex questions, engage in more complex planning, make more inferences, form more hypotheses, find more patterns, develop more new relationships among ideas, and evaluate their own thinking processes more frequently. Many researchers also believe that there is ample evidence to claim that learning to write critically improves students' overall ability to think critically.

Several studies, including one I conducted for my doctoral thesis, confirm that carefully planned intervention strategies can improve the quality of students' thinking when they are writing analytical or argumentative pieces. For example, Marie Scardamalia and David Bereiter tested the effectiveness of an intervention strategy designed to facilitate reflective and critical thought in the planning of essays. They printed sentence openers, such as "A good point on the other side of the argument is that…," on index cards and gave them to students to use when planning their writing. They expected that students would eventually internalize this external aid.

Scardamalia and Bereiter's study, reported in *Literacy, Language and Learning*, found that the essays of students who received the cues displayed significantly more evidence of reflective thinking than those of students who did not receive the cues. This finding held true whether students were cued merely to write more or to reflect, re-evaluate and criticize their own work.

Although writing is an exceptionally powerful means of developing critical thinking skills, I believe that it does this most effectively when integrated with reading, talking and listening. Teachers' chances of helping students learn to think critically are strengthened when we integrate strategies for writing critically with other approaches. And, because there is no evidence to indicate that the simple act of writing improves the ability to think, it's important for teachers to focus on writing strategies that are likely to influence the development of thinking.

This doesn't mean, however, that efforts to use writing to teach thinking need be limited only to analytical writing. Other kinds of writing can also encourage students to form hypotheses, analyze and reflect.

This chapter examines a variety of writing activities that can be used in many content areas to foster critical and reflective thinking. Then, it explores a comprehensive writing program that starts with writing simple definitions and proceeds to writing sustained arguments.

Writing to Think

The activities presented in this section lay the groundwork for the more demanding academic work involved in writing an argumentative essay or research paper. These introductory activities are intended to help students discover not only what they are thinking, but also how, when and why they think as they do.

ADMIT TICKETS AND EXIT PASSES

In addition to helping students focus on various aspects of their learning, these techniques help teachers monitor and adjust instruction as needed.

An admit ticket is an index card given to students at the beginning of a lesson. On it, they record a question, problem or statement related to the course content covered in previous days or for homework.

The tickets can then be used in a variety of ways. We might read and respond to each immediately, or we might select one or two to become the focus of a class discussion. Like ReQuest (see p. 59), this activity gives teachers an opportunity to see what students are thinking. Unlike ReQuest, however, it doesn't focus on a specific reading and, therefore, doesn't limit the discussion.

An exit pass is similar to an admit ticket, but it is completed at the end of a class. On it, students reflect on the day's lesson, commenting on things like what got them thinking, what questions they are left with, and what they would like to think about more—or less. Sometimes, I ask them to reflect on several related lessons or even an entire unit. As they leave the room, I collect their exit passes and read them before we meet again. Doing this often gives me insights into things I need to think about, clarify, explain or demonstrate. These can be addressed in subsequent classes.

QUICK-THINKS

Quick-thinks, sometimes called quick-writes, are reflective writings students complete at critical moments during a lesson. For example, I recently assigned a quick-think during a class discussion of Emerson and individualism. A number of students seemed to have ideas of individualism that I decided would be worthwhile comparing to Emerson's. As a result, I asked the students to take a break and describe or cite an example of individualism to share with the class. This activity gave me a clearer idea of what students were thinking and provided the class with several examples of individualism to classify and contemplate.

LISTING AND CLUSTERING

Asking students to list all the associations they can with a key word, phrase or concept, such as child abuse, is an effective way of encouraging them to begin forming networks of ideas. Although this can be an individual activity, I've found that working in groups stimulates the generation of ideas.

Once ideas have been jotted down, I encourage students to organize these into categories and patterns by making maps or clusters. For example, student teachers in a university class brainstormed associations with the word "authentic" and produced the following map:

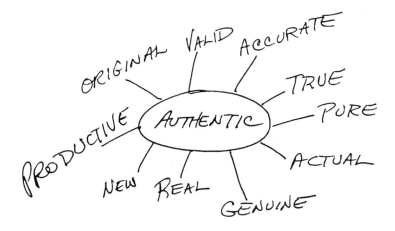

After we generated the map, I asked the students to make connections between words on the map and the concept of authentic achievement, which we had recently discussed. We clustered the terms "new," "original" and "productive" to describe authentic achievement and contrast this with rote learning.

For some students, especially those who like to represent their thinking visually, maps are more flexible concept organizers than formal outlines. When mapping or clustering, students can draw lines, make circles, list and connect ideas, highlight evidence, and show arguments that challenge a thesis.

FOCUSED FREE-WRITES

Focused free-writes help prepare students to think about a topic by activating their background knowledge. They also help teachers assess the extent of this knowledge.

Unlike unfocused free-writes, which place no restrictions on what students can write about, focused free-writes center on a specific topic. For example, when introducing a lesson on commercial bonds in an economics class, I might ask students to take five minutes to jot down everything they can about these financial instruments. To encourage them to focus on generating ideas, I tell them not to worry about spelling, grammar or sentence structure. When the allotted time is up, I ask volunteers to read what they've written and we discuss this as a class.

At intervals while teaching, I often ask students to write letters to me—or someone else, whether this is the principal, a school board member, a character in a story we've read, the school newspaper, or other newspapers and magazines.

If the letters are to me, I might ask students to let me in on their current thinking: what they're learning in other courses or in life, what problems they're trying to solve, what they're discovering about themselves and their own thinking, or what they've learned and been thinking about as a result of what we've covered in class.

If the letters are to characters in stories, I ask students to let the characters know how well they are understood and to pose questions that, if answered, would deepen their understanding of the characters. If the letters are about topics we've been studying, I suggest that students take a position and develop an argument with a view to sending out the letter for publication. I've also asked students to find, read and respond to editorials in newspapers and magazines. After writing their letters, they present the articles to which they're responding to the class, along with their responses.

Submitting a letter for publication in a real newspaper or magazine is highly motivating, especially when it actually appears in print. When this happens, students typically bring their published letters to class where they are posted prominently.

STORY LINES

Using formal or informal logic isn't the only way of developing an argument or persuading an audience to accept a particular point of view. For some readers, a good anecdote has more power to convince than a volume of statistics.

To explore and develop a narrative mode of thought, I ask students to write stories of different kinds. These have included stories that show how they go about thinking when they're trying to persuade a person or group, stories that illustrate how they make important decisions, and stories that illustrate points they wish to make in extended or sustained arguments.

Position papers are documents in which students take—and justify—a stand on an issue. They both prime students to participate in discussions about controversial issues in class and prepare them to write more extensive arguments.

When assigning position papers, I've found that students often ask how long it should be. I first reiterate that the paper is to reflect their opinion about a topic given and include their reasons for holding this opinion. Then I offer guidelines for length, often a range of 150 to 300 words.

RESPONSE AND REFLECTION LOGS

Logs can be used in all disciplines to facilitate reflection, learning and discovery. They enable students to learn more about themselves as thinkers, about how they assess learning and problem-solving tasks, and about their repertoire of strategies for learning and solving problems.

At the outset of the English and social science courses I've taught over the past few years, I ask students to acquire a notebook with about 100 pages. This becomes their log, which we use for writing of many kinds:

— Summaries of texts, such as novels, short stories, essays and editorials.
— Interpretations and re-interpretations of stories and arguments, including justifications for the interpretations.
— Comparisons of characters, stories, arguments and evidence.
— Analysis of characters and arguments.
— Evaluations, both of texts and students' own writing.
— Reflections on learning and problem-solving, including descriptions of reasoning processes or the steps taken in solving a problem.
— Reflections on decisions made and decision-making processes.
— Reflections on knowledge construction and the problems encountered during this process.
— Double-entry journal activities, including responses before and after a reading.

It's worth noting that research indicates that the capacity of individuals to engage in reflection varies widely. For some, doing this seems to be almost instinctive; for others, it is a learned behavior. Teachers need to be alert to this variation and prepared to model how they reflect on their own learning and problem-solving techniques.

When assigning a challenging task in any discipline, whether this involves writing an essay, solving a math problem, conducting a physics experiment, or building a bookshelf, teachers can help students monitor their thinking more effectively by pointing out the importance of paying attention to the process as well as the product. One way of doing this is to ask students to pause from time to time to reflect in their logs on what they are doing. Questions like the following help focus this reflection:

— What steps have you taken to solve the problem?
— Can you think of any other way you might make progress?
— Have you tried—and abandoned—a different approach? If so, why did you abandon that approach and decide to use another?
— Does this task remind you of any other you've ever faced? If so, what was that task and why are you reminded of it?

Once the learning task is complete, I give students time to review their notes and write a more complete description of the thinking process they've just been through.

The process described here illustrates just one process for using learning logs. There are many others. In my experience, learning logs are a more effective tool when the teacher approaches the process with a plan in mind. This plan can include details of how and when they'll be used, and how they'll be evaluated.

THINK-ALOUDS

Although think-alouds require preparation, patience and resources, I can't think of a better window through which to view students' thinking—and their thinking about thinking.

When assigning a think-aloud, I carefully design an appropriate prompt, often a statement or quotation that invites an argumentative essay as a response from the writer. Then, I provide the student with a tape recorder, and send her to a quiet room where she can write the essay and record her responses as she is writing.

Once this phase is complete, the student transcribes her comments word for word, then analyzes and describes the thinking process she went through. This analysis, which includes both an assessment of the effectiveness of their thinking processes and recommendations for improving them, is handed in for review and evaluation.

It's worth noting that a project as detailed, extensive and time-consuming as this isn't practical for all students. Used carefully and selectively, however, the cognitive and meta-cognitive knowledge gained is well worth the effort.

Integrating the Writing Process and Critical Thinking

Over the past 20 years or so, the focus of writing has shifted to process from product. This is an encouraging development for teachers interested in fostering critical thinking because it means that the thinking that goes into the process has become more visible, and intervention strategies can be tailored to fit particular phases. Teachers have an opportunity to design specific strategies to encourage students to do things like generate more ideas, plan more thoroughly, respond helpfully to early drafts of other students' writing, and revise more thoughtfully.

The material that follows describes strategies for integrating the teaching of critical thinking with a process approach to writing sustained arguments. The strategies can be adapted to any subject area.

THE WRITING PROCESS

This discussion assumes that the writing process involves seven phases: pre-writing, planning, drafting, responding, revising and editing, evaluating, and publishing.

Pre-Writing

During this phase, teachers help students prepare for writing by designing activities that encourage them to activate their previous knowledge of a topic, develop new knowledge and make connections between old knowledge and new. These activities include brainstorming, free writing, visualizing, sharing stories, responding to readings related to the topic, talking to others about the topic, and generating relevant thoughts.

Planning

Teachers provide students with the tools, strategies and support they need to organize the knowledge they have gathered and develop a purpose for their writing. During this phase, experienced writers also assess the audience and identify the best way of communicating with or persuading them.

Students can be quite inventive when it comes to planning. Some turn to strategies learned in school, such as preparing an outline, while others activate more personal strategies, such as talking to themselves about how to get organized. Still others find they can visualize their thinking more effectively if they create a map, chart or diagram showing the interconnection of ideas. The TASK procedure can also be used to plan an argumentative essay (see the following chapter).

Drafting

Students translate their plans into an early draft. This phase involves a great deal of thinking, especially if students are reformulating knowledge, making and testing hypotheses, organizing evidence, and testing their claims and those of others.

Responding

Students both seek responses to their own writing and respond to the writing of others. For example, they might work in collaborative groups with response sheets that help them focus on particular aspects of a text. Or individual conferences may be organized to provide guidance and support.

Revising and Editing

Students revise and polish their writing by considering the responses received in the previous phase. This is also the time to check and correct the technical aspects of their writing, such as spelling, grammar and sentence structure.

Evaluating

In accordance with procedures and standards that are often developed by the teacher and students together, the writing is evaluated. It's worth noting that the criteria should be made clear from the outset so that students know what is expected. Although a teacher's thoughtful response to a piece of writing is often valued highly by students, this isn't always necessary. Some teachers encourage students to participate in evaluating their own work by selecting samples of their best work from their portfolio. When they submit these to the teacher for formal evaluation, they explain why they selected the particular pieces.

Publishing

Teachers and students work together to find ways of presenting students' writing to a real audience. Essays may be shared with others in the class, with students in other grades and classes, posted on bulletin boards, bound into a collection, submitted to a newspaper, or presented to an audience in some other form.

Writing That Fosters Critical Thinking

If critical thinking involves reasoned reflection on the meaning of claims about what to believe or what to do, teachers need to encourage students to engage in the kinds of writing that encourage them to do this. Guiding students through the following sequence of writing tasks helps them progress toward their goal, which is to write a complex sustained argument on a controversial issue.

— Describe
— Classify
— Explain
— Summarize
— Compare

One of the keys to helping students through this sequence is to provide models of each category of writing. Students can read and study these models before they start writing on their own.

While guiding students through this sequence is helpful, it's important to remain flexible and alert to their needs. For example, some students may need more practice than others to master a particular skill, or an entire class may need to return to practice a particular troublesome element. Furthermore, it's worth remembering that practicing skills over time is often more effective than concentrating on a particular skill for a short period, then moving on to something else.

DESCRIBE

Although seeing may be believing, language is the mediator that helps us express what we see, both orally and in writing. Clearly, however, expressing what we see can present a challenge. For example, our working vocabulary may limit our power to describe effectively what we have observed. And even if our vocabulary is colossal, words may not satisfactorily convey all the nuances of our observations. In addition, our attitudes and beliefs can color our observations, distorting the images conveyed.

The following activities, which cover a variety of subjects, can be modified to fit students' needs, interests and abilities.

— *Art*: Describe a painting by Rembrandt, Picasso, Manet, Cezanne, etc.
— *Business and economics*: Go to a department store, food store, automobile salesroom, or other place of business. Observe a person or group of individuals shopping, take field notes, and write a description of what you see happening.
— *Biology*: Watch an insect, such as a fly, or group of insects, such as ants, and describe the behavior observed.
— *Chemistry*: Light a candle, observe it burning, and describe what you see.
— *English*: Watch an actor's performance during an episode in a movie several times, take notes on how the actor portrays the character, and describe what you observe.
— *Government*: Sit in on a small claims court proceeding. Observe and describe the process.

- *History*: Attend a municipal council meeting or similar government assembly. Observe and describe what happens during the meeting.
- *Mathematics*: Calculate the total floor area of your house or apartment. Describe how you went about completing this calculation.
- *Music*: Describe one of your favorite pieces of music.
- *Physical education*: Observe a sporting event, such as a baseball or football game, and describe what you see.
- *Physics*: Drop a feather and a rubber ball at the same time from a height of about 10 feet (three meters). Describe your observations.
- *Psychology*: Listen to a conversation between two friends—or enemies—and describe the needs you think the two are expressing through their language and behavior.

It's helpful to keep in mind these criteria when evaluating students' descriptions:

- To what degree has the observer captured the observed?
- Which details are included and to what extent are details described?
- How effectively has the writer used language to convey observations?
- Is the reader drawn into the scene, events or objects described?
- Does the piece have a focus?
- Has the observer been able to keep personal background knowledge and attitudes from clouding the observations?

CLASSIFY

Because we tend to categorize objects and people into groups based on our own experiences, it's important to think critically about categories and categorical claims. This critical awareness can be fostered by suggesting that students develop—and write about—a classification system for a group of objects. Depending on the subject, these objects can include stamps, rocks, dolls, family pictures, sea shells, cartoons, tea cups, leaves, insects, buttons, comics, markers, sports cards, fabric patterns, hats, books and so on.

Students quickly find that this assignment isn't as simple as it seems. They will almost certainly have trouble sorting out which categories to use—and it is their thinking about the process, rather than the act of classifying, that is the key to this assignment. As a result, it's important to encourage them to observe both how they sort and order objects or events and the problems they encounter as they do this.

Questions such as the following help guide students' reflection on the process:

— How did you go about creating categories for the objects you selected to classify?
— What features of the objects did you consider most important when deciding on a classification system?
— Were there any objects that didn't fit readily into a category? If so, what did you do with them?
— Now that you have solved the problem once, what—if anything—would you do differently if you were to face the same problem again?

As students share their reflections on the process with a small group or the class, I encourage them to identify strategies they used.

The following questions can help guide the evaluation of students' reflections:

— Does the writer engage readers by pointing out the purpose and usefulness of the classification system?
— To what degree are categories distinct from one another?
— Does the writer define the principles that make categories different?
— Does the writer claim that all items fit the classification system?
— If all items don't fit into the categories constructed, does the writer let readers know this—or that categories overlap, or that more categories may be needed to fit all the instances?

EXPLAIN

We've all heard people engaged in arguments pause to ask, "What are we talking about?" or "What do you mean by that?" While these questions can be asked during conversations, discussions and debates, writers can't hear readers ask them. As a result, writers must be particularly careful about establishing the meaning of the terms they use.

To help students learn to explain the terms they're using, I often ask them to write definitions that explore and analyze the concept, explain its importance, demonstrate its use, and give examples of its application. Here are examples of concepts from a variety of subject areas that students might be asked to define:

— *Art*: abstract expressionism, casting, chiaroscuro, cubism, draftsperson, etching, glaze, negative space, perspective, pointillism.
— *Business and economics*: bankruptcy, bond, business cycle, common stock, depression, PE ratio, recession, supply and demand, yield.
— *Biology*: disease, ecology, gene, mitosis, niche, osmosis, plant, species.
— *Chemistry*: atomic mass, catalyst, element, ion, polymer, reaction, solution.
— *English*: argument, comedy, epic, grammar, hero, internal monologue, irony, oxymoron, parody, romantic, thesis statement, tragedy, transition.
— *Government*: checks and balances, democracy, due process, judiciary, natural right, republic, tyranny.
— *History*: diplomacy, epoch, inevitability, nationalism, revolution, world view.
— *Mathematics*: algorithm, distributive law, equation, exponent, inequality, order of operations, slope, tangent.
— *Music*: allegro, baroque, cadence, chord, concerto, harmony, jazz, legato, operetta, overtone, rap, sonata form, symphony, waltz.
— *Physical education*: aerobic exercise, balk, birdie, double dribble, foot fault, forward, physical therapy, service line, sports psychology, tailback.
— *Physics*: acceleration, Bernoulli's law, light, nuclear reaction, particle, work.
— *Psychology*: anorexia, behaviorism, dependency needs, depression, intelligence, neurosis, object permanence, personality, psychoanalysis.

Questions like the following can help guide the evaluation of students' papers:

— Has the writer considered the reader's background knowledge?
— Does the explanation engage readers?
— Is the explanation easily followed?
— Does the explanation have a center or focal point?

SUMMARIZE

Students can summarize information using a variety of strategies from cognitive mapping and dialogue profiles to standard outlines. No matter what strategy is selected, however, it's important to encourage students to express key concepts in their own words. Doing this enhances their sense of ownership of the knowledge and helps them make new meanings.

Over the course of a school year, I have asked students in my English classes to summarize many different kinds of texts, including short stories, chapters in novels, expository essays and editorials. These summaries are usually placed in students' learning logs as a resource for discussions, review or writing papers.

I often ask advanced students to extend their summaries to include an analysis and criticism of an argument. Once they've completed this three-phase process—summarize, analyze, criticize—they meet in small groups to share their work and discuss issues that arose as they were reading and writing.

The following questions can help guide the evaluation of summaries:

— Does the summary capture the key ideas?
— Has the writer used his or her own words to express the main ideas?
— Are details kept in the background while main points are in the foreground?
— Is the summary readable?
— Has the writer captured the tone of the original text?

COMPARE

When conducting research or analyzing arguments, students often need to compare objects, concepts and positions. If, for example, they are developing an argument that includes a thesis and an antithesis, they must present these alternative perspectives as they set out both sides of the argument.

As a result, the ability to compare, which involves analyzing both similarities and differences, is an important skill. Here are concepts in a variety of subjects that students might be asked to compare:

— *Art*: photography and painting.
— *Business and economics*: inflation and deflation.
— *Biology*: mitosis and meiosis.
— *Chemistry*: solution and mixture.
— *English*: poetry and verse.
— *Government*: liberal and conservative.
— *History*: socialism and capitalism.
— *Mathematics*: triangle and circle.
— *Music*: rock and rap.
— *Physical education*: football and hockey.
— *Physics*: magnetism and electricity.
— *Psychology*: behaviorism and psychoanalysis.

The following questions can help guide the evaluation of students' comparisons:

— Are the concepts, objects, events or experiences clearly described?
— Are similarities identified and presented clearly?
— Are differences identified and presented clearly?
— Are examples of similarities and differences provided?
— Is the comparison crafted so that readers remain interested?

Planning Lessons

The sequence of activities described in the previous material can be effectively integrated with a process approach to teaching writing.

For example, I once asked students to describe paintings by Rembrandt and used this activity to focus on the pre-writing and planning phases of the writing process. Many students found it interesting when I told them that Ernest Hemingway said he honed his powers of observation by putting into words what he saw in paintings.

As a 15-minute focusing activity, I invited students to view a slide of Rembrandt's *The Anatomy Lesson of Dr. Tulp*, which shows a group of physicians observing a surgeon dissect a cadaver. We talked about what they saw, and I encouraged them to make notes in their learning logs. When the discussion was over, I suggested that they organize their notes into a cognitive map or diagram and include this in their logs. I wanted to show them one way of preparing for the planning phase of the writing process.

To introduce the lesson quickly and link it to the students' lives, I asked them to cite examples of the way their observations influenced their decision-making. And, to tie this to the painting, I asked them to describe how some of their own doctors used observation to diagnose and cure illnesses.

To help students expand their knowledge of any form of writing before actually starting to write, I usually try to provide a model for them to read and discuss. For this lesson, I used John Updike's description of Martin Johnson Heade's 1868 painting *Thunder Storm on Narragansett Bay*. Updike had observed Heade's work in the Metropolitan Museum of Art in New York.

He said:

> The painting is, in fact, strangely idyllic and tranquil. The tawny foreground, whose projecting arm of sand provides the center stage, is sunlit. The two figures walking upon it do not appear to hurry from the coming storm but to saunter; a dim third figure is relaxing the white sail of a beached boat, whose reflection is calmly mirrored in still black water. The seven boats still at sea, and the seven gulls suspended in air, convey a sense of orderly homecoming; the lightning flash is distant, beyond the line of green hills; and the patch of light sky at the left implies that clearing will soon follow the dark clouds lowering their veils of rain harmlessly out to sea;....

We read this paragraph together; then I displayed a print of Heade's painting, enabling students to compare Updike's words with the actual image on the canvas. My goal was to help them understand how the first sentence of his paragraph acts as a frame for the details that follow.

I then displayed another Rembrandt painting, *Aristotle with a Bust of Homer*. In this work, the philosopher, who based most of his ideas on seeing and observing things firsthand, contemplates a bust of the blind poet, who saw things inwardly. Students spent 10 or 15 minutes recording their observations in their logs, paying special attention to whether the technique and approach in this painting were similar to those of the first Rembrandt painting we looked at. They then shared their observations in small groups, and each group prepared a report to present to the class.

Once the groups had reported, the entire class discussed what we were learning about Rembrandt's paintings.

With this groundwork laid, I presented students with the main assignment: to plan and draft a description of Rembrandt's *Storm on the Sea of Galilee*. This painting, which depicts a peaceful Christ crossing a turbulent sea with his fearful disciples, echoes Updike's model describing a stormy seascape.

I displayed the painting and gave students 10 or 15 fifteen minutes to note their observations, and compare this painting with the two Rembrandt works we had viewed earlier. Some of them even made quick sketches of what they saw.

Next, I instructed students to discuss their observations with a partner and work together to create a detailed plan for organizing these into a paper. In the class time remaining, students worked from their plans to begin the first draft of their pieces, which they finished for homework. In subsequent classes, we took the papers through the remaining phases of the writing process.

When the papers were complete, I read and evaluated them. Students stored them in their writing portfolios, and they became part of the end-of-term assessment.

Conclusion

By designing lessons that give students opportunities to use writing to examine and extend their learning, we increase the effectiveness of our teaching. Writing bolsters reflection and writing assignments that are tailored to challenge students progressively foster their capacity to manage complex patterns of thought and to reason reflectively. The next chapter demonstrates how TASK can be applied to the writing of sustained arguments.

THINKING THROUGH WRITING
WITH TASK

With a foundation firmly in place, students are ready to use the skills they've acquired to begin developing their own written arguments. Just as TASK—thesis-analysis-synthesis key—can help students learn to read arguments critically, it can also help them create effective written arguments.

Using TASK to Build Sustained Arguments

A sustained argument asserts—and supports with evidence—a central claim. This may be a fact claim, a causal claim, a predictive claim, an evaluative claim, a moral claim, a policy claim or a mixed claim.

Because identifying and analyzing the causes of events is fundamentally important in work, school and social life, however, I try to focus on causal claims, which assert that certain conditions or circumstances cause—or caused—other conditions or circumstances. "Slavery was the cause of the American Civil War" is an example.

A study conducted by Deanne Kuhn illustrates the need for this focus. In *The Skills of Argument*, Kuhn analyzed the theories people put forward to explain the causes of three urban problems.

The study participants were asked three questions:

— What causes prisoners to return to crime after they're released?
— What causes children to fail in school?

— What causes unemployment?

When supporting their claims, Kuhn found that most people cited pseudo-evidence, such as a sequence of events leading to an effect, rather than genuine evidence, such as data confirming the accuracy of a theory. Furthermore, fewer than half the participants were able to construct counter-arguments to challenge their own theories.

In her book, Kuhn remarked that students rarely, if ever, "take positions and develop arguments to justify them." If this is true, it's up to us, as teachers, to ensure that we provide students with opportunities to do this.

Questions relating to causation can be explored in a variety of disciplines. Here are some examples:

— *Art*: What causes the effect of beauty in art?
— *Business and economics:* Why does business run in cycles?
— *Biology*: How would you explain the forces that drive evolution?
— *Chemistry*: Why do some elements bond while others don't?
— *English*: What makes a good argument?
— *Government*: Why do individuals form governments?
— *History*: What caused the French or American Revolution?
— *Mathematics*: Is mathematics made by man or is it part of nature?
— *Music*: Why is it so difficult to describe music with words?
— *Physical education*: Why do world records continue to be broken?
— *Physics*: Why do objects in motion tend to slow down eventually?
— *Psychology*: What are the roots of gender identity?

Although these questions focus on causal claims, any claim type can be the muscle pumping life into an argument.

After using TASK to analyze arguments, students can apply it to create sustained arguments. Once, when I introduced TASK, one student said, "Oh no! Another way to write a paper that I will never understand!" After going through the process, however, she wrote, "With the format of TASK, I was able to work out my thoughts clearly and simply and easily! My thoughts flowed out and ideas were presented without much effort. That's not to say this method is simple and writes your paper for you. That is very wrong. In order to get the most from this method, one has to be willing to dig for answers and be able to argue with the topic she is writing about. In all, I feel that TASK has improved my writing by supplying me with an outline I can understand as well as allowing me to be creative."

In addition to helping students set goals and establish purposes during the pre-writing phase, TASK helps them plan and organize arguments by stimulating the recall of information and encouraging them to evaluate their claims.

During the actual writing phases, TASK can be used two ways. Students can work through it before starting to write their essays, or they can complete it at the same time they are preparing their early drafts. Either way, successful users usually expand on some of the ideas generated using TASK—and drop others. As a result, when used to guide writing, TASK functions more like a chalkboard than a marble tablet into which truths are chiseled.

THE PHASES OF TASK

To help students identify both their essay-writing strategies and their motivation, I often introduce TASK by encouraging them to reflect on what they currently do when asked to write an argumentative essay. Questions like the following help guide this reflection:

— Do you usually just start writing?
— Do you make an outline?
— Do you talk to yourself, or to others?
— Do you consider the needs and interests of the audience?
— Do you write rough drafts?
— Do you stick closely to the essay structure learned earlier?
— Do you use an approach not mentioned so far?
— Do you use a variety of approaches?
— Do you enjoy the process—or do you find it unpleasant?
— Why do you think you feel this way?

After discussing their current strategies for writing arguments, I guide students through the individual phases of TASK, using brief exercises designed to help them master each phase.

Phase 1—What topic is being judged?

If a topic is clear, concise and well-defined early in the writing process, students can avoid some of the problems that can otherwise crop up as their essays evolve. When writing an essay about music, for example, making a limited but challenging claim about jazz, rock or the blues is more reasonable than arguing about the history of music. If a topic is too broad, students can end up making over-generalized claims about it.

Assigning topics of interest to students or enabling them to select their own topics increases their motivation to plan and write arguments that engage them—and their readers. If students have little feeling for a topic, finding and expressing a purpose is more difficult and their essays tend to lack vitality and meaning.

Phase 2—What basic claim is made about this topic?

Making a decision about which main course to serve at a feast is more enjoyable when the pantry is full of delectable foods than when it's bare. In the same way, deciding on which claim to make about a topic is more enjoyable when there are lots to choose among. Teachers can help students explore a range of claims by planning pre-writing exercises, such as brainstorming, free writing, or talking to a partner.

I try to show students that assertive and challenging claims are more likely to engage the interest of readers. Suppose, for example, that a student wants to write about a proposed plan for simplifying the calculation of income taxes. If the basic claim is that the tax simplification plan is complicated, readers would expect the body of the essay to support this by showing that the proposed simplification isn't simple at all.

If, however, the writer stated that the tax simplification plan should be rejected, this policy claim is more likely to become the basis of an engaging argument designed to convince readers that the plan should be dropped. Examples showing that the new program doesn't really simplify tax computation may very well be presented to support the claim.

Phase 3—Identify the counter-claim: What would a reader who opposes the claim be for or against?

Although students sometimes try to oversimplify opposing claims, identifying an effective counter-claim reveals more thoroughly the core of an opponent's point of view and sets the stage for Phase 4, which involves a thorough examination of the supports for both the claim and the counter-claim. For example, a simple counter-claim for an argument stating that cheating in school is okay if it doesn't hurt anyone might be that cheating is not okay. A more robust, penetrating counter-claim might state that cheating in school is wrong. Even this statement, however, lacks the punch of a specific counter-claim defining what is wrong with cheating: cheaters undermine their own learning and integrity.

Students soon discover that effectively stating a counter-claim helps them anticipate potential challenges to their claim. The tension between claim and counter-claim strengthens the foundation of their argument and heightens readers' interest in it.

To help students practice formulating effective claims and counter-claims, I often give them assignments such as this:

> For each of the following topics, state both a thesis and a forceful antithesis: drug abuse, air quality control, the United Nations, electric automobiles, nuclear energy, surrogate motherhood, computer literacy, health care, poverty, AIDS, television, whaling, a controversial topic of your choice.

Phase 4—What supports the basic claim and the counter-claim? List these supports in separate columns.

When generating a list of supports for both the claim and the counter-claim, students need to be aware of the wide range of resources they have to draw upon. All kinds of claims can be used as sub-claims to build arguments.

At this stage, teachers can also demonstrate that various forms of argument—inductive, deductive and analogical—can be used to build a case in favor of a particular claim. Each form, however, requires a slightly different approach.

An inductive argument, which moves from specific facts to a general conclusion, probably requires research. If, for example, students were building an argument in favor of the policy claim that strict gun control laws should be enacted, they might look for research comparing the rate of violent crime in countries that have strict controls with that in countries that don't.

If time permits, building an inductive argument provides a wonderful opportunity for students to design and carry out their own surveys. When designing their surveys, however, they need to keep the following in mind:

— The questions must be clearly stated.
— Their samples must be representative of the population to which their questions relate.
— Their method of collecting and analyzing data must be unbiased and statistically sound.

Because deductive arguments begin with the general and move toward the specific, it's very important to base these on premises that are rationally sound and avoid making blanket generalizations that can lead to faulty conclusions. Teachers need to provide guidance to help students recognize missing elements and assess their arguments more reasonably.

Analogical reasoning increases the impact of an argument—if the analogy works. Although saying that having a gun in the house is like having a time-bomb in the closet may capture a reader's attention, students need to appreciate that comparisons must be drawn carefully. True analogies—or those with a high degree of truth—add much to an overall argument, but false analogies are likely to weaken the overall impression.

Anecdotes drawn from history and from students' personal lives can also help sustain a claim. When historians make claims about historical cycles, for example, they piece together evidence that may span centuries. This is essentially what Paul Kennedy did in his book, *The Rise and Fall of the Great Powers*. By observing historical patterns, he noted that productive nations that overextend their resources by engaging in wars or conquests risk weakening their national power. Biographers, too, often build claims by piecing together the events of a subject's life. Erik Erikson, for example, did this in his psycho-histories of Martin Luther and Mohandas Gandhi.

Because this phase provides the muscle that supports a writer's argument, careful reasoning is essential. Developing a range of supports takes time, concentration and patience.

Students are more motivated to think through each supporting element when they genuinely care about the purpose of their arguments.

To help them practice this skill, I might give them an assignment like the following:

Select three of the topics for which you identified a claim and a counter-claim in Phases 2 and 3 and work out supports for each.

Phase 5—Does the piece include any unclear, complex or "loaded" language? If so, identify and clarify it.

Just as students need to be alert to this when evaluating the arguments of others, they must be able to identify the need for it in their own writing. And this often depends on the audience. For example, a writer who is developing an argument about behaviorism would be wise to define the term when the piece is intended for a general audience rather than an audience of psychologists.

Furthermore, if this writer is claiming that behavioral techniques can effectively control the aggressive behavior of children, then he might need to explain what "aggressive" means.

Writers also need to identify loaded language and bias. A writer who claims that bankers are capitalist exploiters, for example, may be revealing not only a strong prejudice but also an ideological bias.

Students need to be taught to identify and examine their own biases thoughtfully, and to explain the assumptions on which the bias is based. This helps them gain a deeper understanding of the basis for their judgments.

Phase 6—Evaluate the supports for both the claim and the counter-claim. Identify questionable inferences, irrelevant supports, fallacies and other weaknesses in the argument.

This review involves searching out fallacies of relevance, such as appeals to authority, and weapons of ridicule, such as sarcasm, and finding more effective ways of furthering their arguments.

Phase 7—Do you recognize any assumptions, values or ideological influences in the basic claim or its supports? Identify these and state whether they affect the validity of the claim.

This phase is as useful in writing arguments as it is in reading them. When writing arguments, we may take for granted fundamental concepts that we believe readers accept without explanation. We may, for example, assume that readers have background knowledge about science, history or literature that, in fact, they do not. Or, even more important, we may assume that readers share our ideals, such as the need for peace, or fundamental beliefs, such as in human progress. However, chances are that all readers will not share all our values. As a result, it's a good idea to identify assumptions, values and ideologies and, if necessary, explain and justify them.

In addition, students need to examine the standards they apply when making certain claims. If, for example, a student claims that a movie was terrific, the criteria on which this evaluative claim is based ought to be made clear. What standards did she use to form this opinion? Was it the acting? The direction? The music? The story? The cinematography? If it was one or more of these features, what about them impressed her? What standards of quality are applied to judge the acting, the direction, the story, or any other dimension? Making standards as explicit as possible enables both writers and readers to understand the basis for judgments.

As they analyze assumptions and articulate standards, students generate ideas about the grounds for their belief in the basic claim. These ideas can then be added to the list of reasons that support their thesis.

This phase often involves students in rigorously exploring and testing their own value systems. For example, a student who claims that cheating can be condoned under certain circumstances might find himself examining the underlying values implied by this claim. At what point can cheating no longer be condoned? If one person is allowed to cheat, why isn't everyone, including police officers and judges? If they were, what would our society be like? Whom could we trust?

Teachers need to encourage this kind of questioning, which enables students to assess their own values, an important component of effective critical thinking. Activities like the following can help guide this kind of analysis:

> Decide which of the topics for which you wrote a claim and a counter-claim in Phases 2 and 3 is most controversial and most important, and which is least controversial and least important. For each, explain the assumptions, ideals and values that guided the formulation of your claim and counter-claim.

Phase 8—State the full claim in the following form: Although ... (fill in the counter-claim or one of its strongest supports), ... (fill in the basic claim) because ... (fill in a major cause for belief in the basic claim).

Suppose the basic claim of an argument in favor of gun control states that gun control laws should be passed by the federal government. One of the supports for this claim is that the easy availability of guns increases the likelihood that they will be used on impulse. One of the supports for the counter-claim is that people—not guns—commit violent crimes.

The statement would read:

> Although many opponents of gun control believe that people—not guns—cause violent crimes, gun control laws should be passed by the federal government because the easy availability of guns increases the likelihood that people will use them on impulse to commit violent crimes.

When they combine elements of the TASK procedure into statements like this, students are creating the nucleus of their sustained arguments. Under exam conditions, when the heat is on, using this pattern helps them quickly visualize both the controlling idea and a miniature map to their destination.

To help them internalize this pattern, I often ask them to write similar statements based on the practice exercises we have already completed.

Phase 9—Is the full thesis debatable yet supportable beyond a reasonable doubt, insupportable, or too complex to support?

Making this judgment thoughtfully helps students proceed confidently with the writing of their arguments.

Phase 10—If necessary, revise your statement of the basic claim and repeat the phases of TASK.

If students decide that their thesis doesn't work, now is the time to revise it and work through the phases of TASK once again.

From TASK to Sustained Argument

Once students have been guided through the individual phases of TASK, I suggest that they choose a partner and work through the procedure together. The partners write their arguments separately, then exchange them and compare the results. At this stage, they are usually ready to try the procedure independently.

As we work through TASK, I try to draw students' attention to the realities of the writing process by referring to my own experience using the procedure to compose an argument. As an example, I use an argumentative essay I wrote in favor of stricter gun control legislation. My completed TASK sheet and the essay that resulted are shown in Appendix A.

I begin by talking about why I chose this particular topic—because gun control is an issue that is likely to trouble us all for some time. To emphasize that writing is a dynamic process that involves constant revisions, I talk about my own struggle to complete the phases of TASK. For example, I found that the content changed as I wrote—and rewrote—the essay. At one point, as I was doing some additional reading at the library, I came across statistical and historical information that it seemed important to include. I also read many arguments both for and against gun control that helped me identify potential counter-arguments.

I also stress that, as I revised, the structure of the essay changed. In fact, it didn't assume its current form until about the third draft. By the time I'd written the second draft, however, I was pretty certain that I'd open with some specific examples of deaths that might not have occurred if guns hadn't been readily available. The examples were drawn from newspaper and magazine reports. In addition, early versions included the "Although..." statement of the thesis drawn from Phase 8 of TASK, which I eventually decided to drop.

And, after reviewing Phase 5, which deals with complex terms, I added a definition of gun control.

By modeling what I went through, I hope to make it clear that writing an essay using the TASK procedure isn't a linear process. It's more like doing a painting that begins with a penciled sketch and evolves as the canvas is filled in.

Evaluating Sustained Arguments

To ensure that students understand how their essays will be evaluated, we talk about expectations beforehand and I distribute the scoring guide shown on the following page. It rates various elements on a sliding scale and combines analytical and holistic evaluation.

The scoring scale ranges from 4 to 10. The total of the analytical elements can, therefore, range from 40 to 100. The guide also includes a score for overall impression, which usually reflects the sum of the analytical features.

This guide is designed for use by both the students and the teacher. I often ask students, for example, to evaluate one another's essays in groups of three that include one high-achiever, one average achiever and one low-achiever. Based on these responses, students have an opportunity to revise their pieces before storing them in their portfolios or handing them in for my evaluation.

Grappling with Controversial Issues

Several years ago, I began to encourage students to focus on controversial issues by introducing research projects that culminated in the writing of a paper. For example, after reading Paul Kennedy's *Preparing for the Twenty-First Century*, I designed a theme on the 21st century. We discussed the fact that most of today's students will actually live their lives in the next century, and talked about the kinds of problems they are likely to face when they are in their 20s, 30s, 40s and beyond. I then suggested that they investigate and report on one of these.

Here are the instructions they were given:

Explore various positions that might be adopted with respect to a controversial issue and examine the reasons

Scoring Guide: Argumentative Essay

*Name*_____

For each quality, circle the number that most nearly describes this paper.

1. Sophistication of Claim—Scope, Depth and Clarity
   Shallow   *Comprehensive*
   4   5   6   7   8   9   10

2. Number of Supports
   Few (1)   *Many (4 or more)*
   4   5   6   7   8   9   10

3. Elaboration of Supports
   Little   *Considerable*
   4   5   6   7   8   9   10

4. Concreteness and Specificity of Evidence
   Bland, general   *Vivid, specific*
   4   5   6   7   8   9   10

5. Counter-Claim(s)
   Weak   *Thorough*
   4   5   6   7   8   9   10

6. Sense of Serious Critical Thinking
   Unconsidered   *Reflective, fair*
   4   5   6   7   8   9   10

7. Coherence of Argument
   Disordered   *Cohesive*
   4   5   6   7   8   9   10

8. Planning
   Rudimentary   *Clear*
   4   5   6   7   8   9   10

9. Paragraph Development—
   Topic Sentences, Variety, Transitions
   Weak   *Strong*
   4   5   6   7   8   9   10

10. Mechanics—Grammar, Sentence Structure, Etc.
    Needs much attention   *Needs little attention*
    4   5   6   7   8   9   10

    TOTAL ____

Overall Impression
   Needs much work   *Superb*
   4   5   6   7   8   9   10

Comments

for advocating each position. This will require extensive research. After examining alternative views and documenting their rationale, indicate in your paper which position you find most reasonable.

My role was to function as both a retriever and a watchdog, helping students gather information and ensuring that they stayed on track. To ensure that the necessary resources would be available, they selected from a pool of topics for which articles and books were available in our school library or in neighboring libraries. From this pool, each student initially selected five, then narrowed this to one by pulling a number from a box. This procedure also ensured fairness in the event that more than one student chose the same issue.

The collaboration of the school librarian was critical to the success of this project. She stocked shelves with books on controversial issues and developed files of publications and news clippings on these issues. I made sure the students had plenty of library time to begin their investigation.

Students eventually selected issues that focused on questions like the following:

— How should we prepare to care for the aged?
— How can children of divorced parents be empowered to cope with their families?
— How can we keep our oceans free of pollution?
— What will become of our water resources in the 21st century?
— Should our government take more—or less—direct action to control population growth?
— What role will technology play in the schools of the 21st century?
— Should the death penalty be abolished?
— Can or should human intelligence be increased?
— How are we to judge what is right and wrong, good or bad as we make decisions that affect our futures?
— Will our country's influence rise or fall in the 21st century?
— Will corporations have more social and political power in the 21st century?

As part of the process, students used the TASK procedure to formulate their argument and counter-arguments, organize evidence and counter-evidence, and plan the paper's structure. The paper itself, which was to be about 2,500 words, was to follow established guidelines.

From the beginning, evaluation criteria, which were adapted from the scoring guide shown previously, were made clear. For this project, I combined Categories 2 (Number of Supports) and 3 (Elaboration of Supports) into a single category labeled "Strength of Supports." To emphasize the importance of careful, thorough research and appropriate documentation, I added a category evaluating the use of references.

After completing the written phases of the project, students prepared an oral presentation. This involved outlining the problem they examined, the results of their inquiry, alternative viewpoints on the issue, the solution or perspective they decided to adopt, and the reasons for doing so. The depth of analysis in both the written and oral presentations and the lively class discussions that followed the oral presentations were delightful. I could see students grappling in thoughtful ways with authentic problems that will affect their lives.

Conclusion

Once students have acquired a foundation for critical thinking and tools they can use to conduct extended inquiries, we can provide them with opportunities to write sustained arguments, one of the most effective strategies for developing their ability to think critically. This ability equips them to take advantage of opportunities at school, at work and in the community to take positions on issues and develop arguments to support them, a skill that helps them live an examined life.

. . . .

EPILOGUE

Books on education reform abound. Teacher education programs buzz with talk of restructuring and revitalizing classrooms. Administrators advocate and encourage change. But authentic and enduring transformation in education comes more often than not from committed classroom teachers. If teachers like Al and his colleagues, the fictional group whose story was told in the introduction, work toward the goal of teaching for thinking, then more critical thinkers and reflective learners will emerge from our schools.

Imagine how the scenario might have played out at Al's school. With a mixture of enthusiasm and some initial resentment, Al's colleagues frame a vision of teaching for thinking. To the satisfaction of many faculty members, the new principal plays an active role in successfully persuading teachers in each discipline to embrace this vision.

The faculty adopts a three-year plan designed to integrate critical thinking into all content areas, including physical education, music and art. During the first year, this process involves a series of workshops designed to clarify how their vision of teaching for thinking can be realized by departments and by individual teachers. During the workshops, they plan to work with one another and with specialists to redesign the curriculum so that critical and reflective thinking becomes an integral part of students' learning. The principal and representatives of the faculty introduce the plan to parents and win their support. To evaluate their success, several departments decide to use portfolio assessment, and arrange to measure changes in students' ability to think critically by comparing their results with those of students in a similar school.

Despite their enthusiastic plans, Al and his colleagues acknowledge what lies ahead. Bringing about this kind of fundamental change in the educational ethos of an entire faculty requires hard work and patience. The teachers at Adams High will need sensitive leadership, courage, creative cooperation and stamina if they are to achieve the transformation they're seeking. Guiding their struggle is the knowledge that developing students who are critical thinkers and reflective learners will imbue their teaching with greater meaning.

This vision need not remain in the realm of fiction. A single teacher in a single classroom can certainly pursue the ideal of teaching for thinking. But this ideal is more likely to be realized when our colleagues share the vision and work with us—and the students—to create a classroom environment in which transforming knowledge is more important than merely transmitting it.

APPENDIX A

Thesis-Analysis-Synthesis Key

1. What topic is being judged?
   Gun control.

2. What basic claim is made about this topic?
   A network of federal gun-control measures should be enacted to limit the availability and firepower of guns, while increasing their safety.

3. Identify a counter-claim: What would a reader who opposes the claim most likely be for or against?
   Citizens should be able to buy and keep guns of any kind.

4. What supports the basic claim and the counter-claim? List these supports in separate columns.

Basic Claim Supports	Counter-Claim Supports
40-45% of homes have guns.	*Guns don't kill. People do.*
16 children and teenagers shot to death every day.	
Guns are 2nd leading cause of death for people 10-34.	
If citizens can't control abuse, legislation needed.	*Citizens should solve gun problems within states.*
Licensing supports knowledgeable use.	
Can't afford to address underlying problems.	*Roots of violence lie in deeper social problems.*
Second amendment applies only to militia.	*Constitutional right to bear arms.*
Limiting access limits criminal misuse.	*Gun-control laws don't work.*
Research shows controls are effective.	*Research is flawed.*
Limiting firepower reduces killing power.	*Hunters need semi-automatic rifles.*
Improved safety measures reduce accidents and theft.	*Manufacturing costs would rise.*

5. Does the piece include any unclear, complex or "loaded" language? If so, identify and clarify it.

Gun control means different things to different people. Despite efforts to clarify meaning, multiple meanings readers bring to the argument will probably contribute to some degree of confusion. In addition, the Second Amendment is interpreted differently by those who favor gun control and those who oppose it.

6. Evaluate the supports for both the claim and the counter-claim. Identify questionable inferences, irrelevant supports, fallacies and other weaknesses in the argument.

Although opponents of gun control argue that studies of the effects of gun control are flawed, many reasonably designed studies indicate that limiting access to guns reduces violence with guns. However, even reputable studies such as Dr. John Sloan's include variables that are difficult to control. These perceived weaknesses make many studies more difficult to interpret. Additional well-designed studies are needed. Furthermore, at this point in the research on gun control, a meta-analysis of such studies might be beneficial and more convincing.

7. Do you recognize any assumptions, values or ideological influences in the basic claim or its supports? Identify these and state whether they affect the validity of the claim.

Assumption and value: The freedom to bear arms is not worth the loss of life to which this freedom contributes. Most sensible citizens have a right and obligation to regain control of the destructive power of guns in the hands of a minority.

8. State the full claim in the following form: Although ... (fill in the counter-claim or one of its strongest supports), ... (fill in the basic claim) because ... (fill in a major cause for belief in the basic claim).

Although some people say, "Guns don't kill; people do," it's time to enact federal laws to limit access to guns and make ownership safer because guns are destroying us and our children.

9. Is the full thesis debatable yet supportable beyond a reasonable doubt, insupportable, or too complex to support?

The full thesis appears debatable yet supportable.

10. If necessary, revise your statement of the basic claim and repeat the phases of TASK.

A three-year-old boy was hit in the head by a bullet as he slept on the couch in his living room. An eight-year-old boy was shot in the stomach when he was caught in an exchange of gunfire. During recess, a middle school girl was shot while out on the playing field. All died.

According to several studies, a gun can be found in 40 to 45 per cent of all American homes, a pistol in one of every four. Those estimating that there are 70 million handguns in homes are hitting the target. With all this firepower available, 16 children are killed every day with a gun, according to the National Center for Health Statistics.

To curtail violence with guns, the United States needs federal gun control laws that limit both access to guns and their firepower, while making ownership and use much safer.

The first step in limiting access should be the passage of federal legislation that requires every person owning a gun to have a license. As part of the licensing process, the waiting period before a gun can be purchased should be 21 days. During this time, a fingerprint check should be conducted. In addition, all gun owners should be required to pass carefully monitored, rigorous written and performance tests to demonstrate knowledge of guns, gun regulations and gun functions. Drivers of automobiles must already pass tests like this. Owners of guns, which are second only to vehicles as the killing agents of people in the 10 to 34 age range, should also be required to demonstrate their knowledge of gun use. After clearing the screening process and passing the tests, those wanting to own and use a gun would be issued a license to purchase no more than one gun a month. The development and administration of these tests, the issuance of the licenses, and provisions for periodic recertification would be supervised by the Bureau of Alcohol, Tobacco and Firearms.

While requiring owners to be licensed will undoubtedly reduce the misuse of guns, a second step must limit access to formidable firepower by passing federal legislation that prohibits the manufacture, distribution and sale to the public of all automatic and semi-automatic assault weapons and all magazines of more than 10 rounds for any weapon. Hunters don't require battlefield weaponry outfitted with 125-round drum magazines.

While these limits to access, use and firepower are necessary, they won't reduce the dangers to which American citizens are daily exposed. As a third step, safety features must be implemented to reduce the violent and tragic misuse of guns. This law would require all newly manufactured guns to function only for the licensed individual purchasing that gun. The technology already exists to ensure this personalization through chip-to-chip or fingerprint recognition. Manufacturers would be compelled to innovate. To increase the safety of earlier model guns, the law should require that they be outfitted with a trigger lock. Individuals who fail to install suitable locks would be charged with negligence in the case of injury or death arising from the gun's use.

Opponents counter that such a network of gun-control regulations is unconstitutional, that it doesn't get at the roots of the problem, or that it simply won't work. These objections wither under scrutiny.

Although the Supreme Court has clearly upheld the constitutionality of gun control, opponents often argue that, in the 1770s and 1780s, Americans fought for and won the right to bear arms, which is enshrined in the language of the Second Amendment: "A well regulated Militia, being necessary to the Security of a free State, the right of the people to keep and bear arms shall not be infringed." However, the Second Amendment was intended to permit state militias, not individuals, to bear arms. At the time the Constitutional Convention was debating the Second Amendment, legislators were not as concerned with individual rights to bear arms as they were with the rights of states to protect themselves from the new "United States," which had the authority to raise an army. No federal court has ever overturned a gun-control law for violating the Second Amendment.

Even if we grant that the Second Amendment could be interpreted to mean that individuals have the right to bear arms, we no longer live in 1775 when imperious British authorities sought to remove each citizen's firearms to suppress rebellion. Since then, America has changed dramatically. Large populations of citizens from diverse cultures are now concentrated into often competing and volatile communities where poverty contributes to desperation and aggression. With changes in values and education over the past 200 years, individuals appear to have lost some of their capacity to tolerate frustration, control their impulses, and work and wait for gratification. If inner controls cannot be exercised, then—for the sake of civilization—controls must be exercised from without. One way to exercise control is to prevent the sale of guns and ammunition to those who are ready to explode. If Americans must make sure that all gun owners are licensed and that access to guns and firepower is reasonably controlled, then this is the price we must now pay for many of the same rights won in the Revolution: life, liberty and the pursuit of happiness.

Although opponents of gun control may concede that the level of violence in American cities has become unconscionable, they say it has nothing to do with guns. The problem, they say, is people—not guns. If Americans want to address deeply rooted social and economic problems in our cities, say the opponents of gun control, they must dig to get at the roots.

What are these roots? Poverty, unemployment, poor education, psychological dysfunction, drugs. The roots of these social and economic problems are embedded in American history. The most violent centers of crime are populated by men and women unable or unwilling to find productive work. Frequently, poverty has been their inheritance. Disengagement from education—dropping out of school—has resulted from the perception that schools are meaningless or present a path to a way of life that has little appeal.

The cycle of poverty and miseducation means that psychological problems such as weak impulse control, aggression, depression and blurred ego boundaries abound. Few individuals suffering from psychological dysfunction seek help in an environment where help is rare. Possessed by disquieting frustration and rage, some find solace in drugs, some in gangs. But the culture of drugs and gangs usually breeds more conflict and greater demands for satisfaction—with little or no concern about the effects of one's behavior on others. Crack, for example, diminishes human judgment. Getting and taking the drug becomes an all-consuming goal. If guns can help in the battle to protect a gang's pride and turf or to get drugs—or to keep the profits from them—guns will be used.

"So, address the underlying problems," say the critics of gun control, "and leave us our right to bear arms." Without doubt, these problems must be addressed quickly and broadly. But the underlying problems are so complex and deeply rooted that their solution will take many years and billions of dollars. Thousands—even tens of thousands—of people are yet to die from gunshot wounds intended and random. Many will be children at play or in school classrooms and corridors, men doing errands and chores, women merely walking down a quiet street.

Finally, opponents of gun control say that gun-control laws simply don't work. However, researchers have repeatedly shown that fewer homicides with guns take place in regions that have strict gun-control measures. In a study comparing Vancouver, British Columbia, with Seattle, Washington, and published in the *New England Journal of Medicine*, Dr. John Sloan attributed the much lower rate of gun-related homicide in Vancouver to its effective gun-control legislation. While opponents of gun control find flaws in the design of research like this, the fact remains that the rate of homicides caused by guns is much lower in countries with strict gun regulations, such as England and Japan.

Yes, people kill—not guns. But if the people have become reckless, deadly in their own dens, heedless of sensible internal restraint, then external constraints become a reasonable alternative. And one of the most effective, efficient ways to impose constraints is to limit access to guns and their firepower while taking steps to increase their safety in the home. At the time of British domination of the Americas, a disarmed populace was an invitation to tyranny. But, Americans are no longer the Minute Men at Concord fighting for freedom from an oppressive British monarchy. To curtail a new tyranny— meaningless deaths from gunshots—we must license all gun owners just as we now license all drivers, limit firepower, and insist on stronger safety requirements for gun owners. By enacting a network of federal gun-control measures, we can end the shoot-out that is taking place in our cities and make our homes safer.

. . . .

RESOURCES

Additional Reading

Baron, J. *Thinking and Deciding*. Cambridge, England: Cambridge University Press, 1994.

Bernstein, R.J. *Beyond Objectivism and Relativism: Science, Hermeneutics, and Praxis*. Philadelphia, Penn.: University of Pennsylvania Press, 1983.

Beyer, B. *Developing a Thinking Skills Program*. Boston, Mass.: Allyn & Bacon, 1988.

Costa, A. *Developing Minds: A Resource Book for Teaching Thinking* (Vols. 1 & 2). Alexandria, Va.: Association for Supervision and Curriculum Development, 1991.

Costa, A.L. & F. Lawrence. *Techniques for Teaching Thinking*. Pacific Grove, Calif.: Critical Thinking Books & Software, 1989.

Ennis, R. *Critical Thinking*. Upper Saddle River, N.J.: Prentice Hall, 1996.

Flower, L., D.L. Wallace, L. Norris & R.E. Burnett. *Making Thinking Visible: Writing, Collaborative Planning, and Classroom Inquiry*. Urbana, Ill.: National Council of Teachers of English, 1994.

Gardner, H. *Frames of Mind: The Theory of Multiple Intelligences*. New York, N.Y.: Basic Books, 1985.

Govier, T. *A Practical Study of Argument*. Belmont, Calif.: Wadsworth Publishing, 1995.

Halpern, D.F. *Thought and Knowledge: An Introduction to Critical Thinking.* Hillsdale, N.J.: Lawrence Erlbaum, 1995.

Kahane, H. *Logic and Contemporary Rhetoric: The Use of Reason in Everyday Life.* Belmont, Calif: Wadsworth Publishing, 1992.

Lipman, M. *Thinking in Education.* New York, N.Y.: Cambridge University Press, 1991.

Olson, C.B. *Thinking Writing: Fostering Critical Thinking through Writing.* New York, N.Y..: HarperCollins, 1992.

Paul, R., A.J.A. Binker, D. Martin & K. Adamson. *Critical Thinking Handbook: High School.* Rohnert Park, Calif.: Center for Critical Thinking and Moral Critique, 1989.

Perkins, D. *Knowledge as Design.* Hillsdale, N.J.: Lawrence Erlbaum, 1986.

Perkins, D., E. Jay & S. Tishman. "Beyond Abilities: A Dispositional Theory of Thinking. In *Merrill-Palmer Quarterly.* Vol. 39, no. 1: 1993.

Rottenberg, A. *Elements of Argument.* New York, N.Y.: St. Martin's Press, 1994.

Siegel, H. *Educating Reason.* London, England: Routledge, 1988.

Sternberg, R.J. *The Triarchic Mind: A New Theory of Human Intelligence.* New York, N.Y.: Viking, 1988.

Swartz, R. & S. Parks. *Infusing the Teaching of Critical and Creative Thinking into Content Instruction.* Pacific Grove, Calif.: Critical Thinking Books & Software, 1994.

Swartz, R. & D.N. Perkins. *Teaching Thinking: Issues and Approaches.* Pacific Grove, Calif.: Critical Thinking Books & Software, 1990.

Tishman, S., D. Perkins & E. Jay. *The Thinking Classroom: Learning and Teaching in a Culture of Thinking.* Boston, Mass.: Allyn & Bacon, 1995.

Toulman, S. *The Uses of Argument.* Cambridge, England: Cambridge University Press, 1958.

Whimbey, A. *Analytical Reading and Reasoning.* Stamford, Conn.: Innovative Sciences, 1982.

Resource Centers

Center for Critical Thinking
Christopher Newport University
50 Shoe Lane, Newport News, Va. 23606

Center for Critical Thinking and Moral Critique
Sonoma State University
1801 E. Cotati Ave., Rohnert Park, Calif. 94928

Centre for Research in Critical Thinking
University of East Anglia
Norwich, England NR47TJ

Institute for Critical Thinking
Montclair State University
Upper Montclair, N.J. 07043

National Center for Teaching Thinking
815 Washington Street, Ste. 8, Newtonville, Mass. 02160

Project Zero
Graduate School of Education
Longfellow Hall, 3rd Floor
Harvard University, Cambridge, Mass. 02138

Thinking Works
P.O. Box 468, St. Augustine, Fla. 32085

Simulations and Controversial Issues

Interact
Box 997, Lakeside, Calif. 92040

Opposing Viewpoints
Greenhaven Press, Inc.
P.O. Box 289009, San Diego, Calif. 92198-9009

Taking Sides: Clashing Views on Controversial Issues
Dushkin Publishing Group Inc.
Sluice Dock, Guilford, Conn. 06437

. . . .

REFERENCES

Ayer, A.J. *Language, Truth and Logic.* New York, N.Y.: Dover Publications, 1952.

Beach, R. *A Teacher's Introduction to Reader-Response Theories.* Urbana, Ill: National Council of Teachers of English, 1993.

Bernstein, R.J. *Beyond Objectivism and Relativism: Science, Hermeneutics, and Praxis.* Philadelphia, Pa.: University of Pennsylvania Press, 1983.

Bloom, B.S., et al. *Taxonomy of Educational Objectives, Handbook I: Cognitive Domain.* New York, N.Y.: Longmans, 1956.

Brown, A.L., A.S. Palincsar & B.B. Armbruster. "Instructing Comprehension-Fostering Activities in Interactive Learning Situations." In *Theoretical Models and Processes of Reading,* 4th Ed. (R.B. Ruddell, M.R. Ruddell & H. Singer, Eds.). Newark, Del.: International Reading Association, 1994.

Calfee, R.C., K.L. Dunlap & A.Y. Wat. "Authentic Discussion of Texts in Middle Grade Schooling: An Analytic-Narrative Approach." In *Journal of Reading.* Vol. 37, no. 7: 1994.

Costa, A. *Cognitive Coaching: A Foundation for Renaissance Schools.* Norwood, Md: Christopher-Gordon Publishers, 1994.

Costa, A. *Developing Minds: A Resource Book for Teaching Thinking* (Vols. 1 and 2). Alexandria, Va: Association for Supervision and Curriculum Development, 1991.

Ennis, R. "Goals for a Critical Thinking Curriculum." In *Developing Minds: A Resource Book for Teaching Thinking: Volume 1.* (A.

Costa, Ed.) Alexandria, Va.: Association for Supervision and Curriculum Development, 1991.

Ennis, R. *Critical Thinking*. Upper Saddle River, N.J.: Prentice Hall, 1996.

Erikson, E. *Young Man Luther*. New York, N.Y.: W.W. Norton, 1958.

Erikson, E. *Gandhi's Truth: On the Origins of Militant Nonviolence*. New York, N.Y.: W.W. Norton, 1969.

Fromm, E. *The Art of Loving*. New York, N.Y.: Harper & Row, 1956.

Hirsch, E.D. Jr. *Cultural Literacy: What Every American Needs to Know*. Boston, Mass.: Houghton Mifflin, 1987.

Hunkins, F. *Teaching Thinking through Effective Questioning*. Norwood, Md.: Christopher-Gordon Publishers, 1995.

Keefer, M. Judging the Quality of Reflective Discussion. Paper presented at the annual meeting of the American Educational Research Association. New York, N.Y., April 1996.

Kennedy, P.M. *The Rise and Fall of the Great Powers: Economic Change and Military Conflict from 1500 to 2000*. New York, N.Y.: Random House, 1988.

Kennedy, P.M. *Preparing for the Twenty-first Century*. New York, N.Y.: Random House, 1993.

Kuhn, D. *The Skills of Argument*. Cambridge, England.: Cambridge University Press, 1991.

Kuhn, T. *The Structure of Scientific Revolutions*. Chicago, Ill.: University of Chicago Press, 1962.

Manzo, A.V. "The ReQuest Procedure." In *Journal of Reading*. Vol. 13, no. 2: 1969.

McPeak, J.E. *Critical Thinking and Education*. Oxford, England: Martin Robertson, 1981.

Mehan, H. *Learning Lessons: Social Organization in the Classroom*. Cambridge, Mass.: Harvard University Press, 1979.

Ogle, D. "K-W-L: A Teaching Model That Develops Active Reading of Expository Text." In *The Reading Teacher*. Vol. 39, no. 6: 1986.

Paul, R., A.J.A. Binker, D. Martin & K. Adamson. *Critical Thinking Handbook: High School*. Rohnert Park, Calif.: Center for Critical Thinking and Moral Critique, 1989.

Piaget, J. & B. Inhelder. *The Psychology of the Child*. New York, N.Y.: Basic Books, 1969.

Rosenblatt, L.M. *The Reader, the Text, the Poem: The Transactional Theory of the Literary Work*. Carbondale, Ill.: Southern Illinois University Press, 1978.

Rosenblatt, L.M. "The Transactional Theory of Reading and Writing." In *Theoretical Models and Processes of Reading*. 4th Ed. (R.B. Ruddell, M.R. Ruddell & H. Singer, Eds.). Newark, Del.: International Reading Association, 1994.

Scardamalia, M. & C. Bereiter. "Development of Dialectical Processes in Composition." In *Literacy, Language, and Learning*. (D. Olson, N. Torrance & A. Hildyard, Eds.) Cambridge, England: Cambridge University Press, 1986.

Spolin, V. *Improvisation for the Theatre*. Evanston, Ill.: Northwestern University Press, 1963.

Stanovich, K. "Reconceptualizing Intelligence: Dysrationalia as an Intuition Pump." In *Educational Researcher*. Vol. 23, no. 4: 1994.

Stauffer, R.G. *Directing Reading Maturity as a Cognitive Process*. New York, N.Y.: Harper & Row, 1969.

Toulman, S. *The Uses of Argument*. Cambridge, England: Cambridge University Press, 1958.

Unrau, N. "The TASK of Reading and Writing: A Study of the Effects of a Procedural Facilitator on the Construction of Arguments. Unpublished doctoral dissertation, University of California, Berkeley, 1989. (University Microfilms, No. 9028702).

Unrau, N. "The TASK of Reading (and Writing) Arguments: A Guide to Building Critical Literacy." In *Journal of Reading*. Vol. 35, no. 6: 1992.

Unrau, N. & R. Ruddell. "Interpreting Texts in Classroom Contexts." In *Journal of Adolescent and Adult Literacy*. Vol. 39, no. 1: 1995.

Updike, J. "Heade Storms." In *The New York Review of Books*. Vol. 42, no. 2: January 12, 1995.

Verriour, P. *In Role: Teaching and Learning Dramatically*. Markham, Ontario: Pippin Publishing, 1994.

Vygotsky, L. *Mind in Society* (M. Cole, S. Scribner, V.J. Steiner & E. Souberman, Eds. and Trans.). Cambridge, Mass.: Harvard University Press, 1978.

Vygotsky, L. *Thought and Language.* (A. Kozulin, Ed. and Trans.). Cambridge, Mass.: MIT Press, 1986. (Original work published 1934.)

Zeitz, C. The Development of Conversational Reasoning Skills in the Domain of Literature. Paper presented at the annual meeting of the American Educational Research Association. New York, N.Y., April 1996.